FLOYD CLYMER'S MOTORCYCLIST'S LIBRARY

The Book of the
250 cc BSA

A Practical Handbook covering all models from 1954 to 1970

Arthur Lupton, M.I.Mech.E.

ANNOUNCEMENT

By special arrangement with the original publishers of this book, Sir Isaac Pitman & Son, Ltd., of London, England, we have secured the exclusive publishing rights for this book, as well as all others in THE MOTORCYCLIST'S LIBRARY.

Included in THE MOTORCYCLIST'S LIBRARY are complete instruction manuals covering the care and operation of respective motorcycles and engines; valuable data on speed tuning, and thrilling accounts of motorcycle race events. See listing of available titles elsewhere in this edition.

We consider it a privilege to be able to offer so many fine titles to our customers.

FLOYD CLYMER
Publisher of Books Pertaining to Automobiles and Motorcycles

2125 W. PICO ST.   LOS ANGELES 6, CALIF.

INTRODUCTION

Welcome to the world of digital publishing ~ the book you now hold in your hand, while unchanged from the original edition, was printed using the latest state of the art digital technology. The advent of print-on-demand has forever changed the publishing process, never has information been so accessible and it is our hope that this book serves your informational needs for years to come. If this is your first exposure to digital publishing, we hope that you are pleased with the results. Many more titles of interest to the classic automobile and motorcycle enthusiast, collector and restorer are available via our website at **www.VelocePress.com**. We hope that you find this title as interesting as we do.

NOTE FROM THE PUBLISHER

The information presented is true and complete to the best of our knowledge. All recommendations are made without any guarantees on the part of the author or the publisher, who also disclaim all liability incurred with the use of this information.

TRADEMARKS

We recognize that some words, model names and designations, for example, mentioned herein are the property of the trademark holder. We use them for identification purposes only. This is not an official publication.

INFORMATION ON THE USE OF THIS PUBLICATION

This manual is an invaluable resource for the classic **BSA** enthusiast and a "must have" for owners interested in performing their own maintenance. However, in today's information age we are constantly subject to changes in common practice, new technology, availability of improved materials and increased awareness of chemical toxicity. As such, it is advised that the user consult with an experienced professional prior to undertaking any procedure described herein. While every care has been taken to ensure correctness of information, it is obviously not possible to guarantee complete freedom from errors or omissions or to accept liability arising from such errors or omissions. Therefore, any individual that uses the information contained within, or elects to perform or participate in do-it-yourself repairs or modifications acknowledges that there is a risk factor involved and that the publisher or its associates cannot be held responsible for personal injury or property damage resulting from the use of the information or the outcome of such procedures.

One final word of advice, this publication is intended to be used as a reference guide, and when in doubt the reader should consult with a qualified technician.

Preface

PRODUCTION was resumed after the war with the "C" group of 250 cm^3 models, which progressed steadily in design, being fitted in turn with telescopic front forks and then plunger rear suspension. Eventually the generator took the form of an engine-speed alternator, with rectifier for battery charging, superseding the chain-driven dynamo of previous years. By 1956, the rear suspension had changed to the "swinging arm" type, with hydraulically damped suspension units.

A complete re-design in 1958 culminated in the production of the 250 Star, which included for the first time on a B.S.A. 250 c.c. machine, unit construction of the engine and gearbox.

It would not be possible, nor even desirable, to attempt to cover the whole sequence of these lightweight models in a book of this size, and the First Edition dealt solely with those 250 c.c. machines manufactured between 1954 and 1962. The machines concerned were the S.V. Model C10L, O.H.V. Model C11G, its successor the C12, and the completely re-designed 250 Star-Model C15. The latter was also produced as a Sport Star Model C15SS, a Trials Star Model C15T, and a Scrambles Model C15S.

The trials and scrambles machines were discontinued after 1964, but the C15 Star and its sports version (now known as the Sportsman, instead of the SS80 Sport Star) underwent a process of steady development. Further improvements to the C15 Star engine (mainly to the lower half) took place towards the end of 1966 and these engines are identified by the series C15G. At the same time the Sportsman was discontinued. The production of the C15 Star was continued throughout 1967, together with that of an entirely new version of the 250 c.c. class having a high performance engine based on an extremely successful model of larger engine capacity, with a quickly-detachable rear wheel, 12-volt lighting, and other features.

The new 250 c.c. models were known as the Barracuda (model C25) and the Starfire (model B25), differing only slightly in specification to suit different markets. Production of the C15 Star ceased towards the end of 1967 and the Starfire alone continued until 1970. Instructions applicable to all recent 250 c.c. models have now been added to this maintenance handbook.

The author would like to thank the directors of B.S.A. Motor Cycles Ltd. for providing technical information and for permission to reproduce certain B.S.A. illustrations.

A.G.L.

Contents

	Preface	iii
1	B.S.A. Lubrication	1
2	General Maintenance	11
3	The Clutch and Gearbox	41
4	Decarbonizing the Engine	66
5	Dismantling and Reassembly of the Engine	78
6	Steering and Suspension	91
7	The Electrical Equipment	104
8	The Carburettor	115
	Index	122

1 B.S.A. Lubrication

It has been established practice for many years for all B.S.A. engines to employ dry-sump lubrication. In this system, the lubricating oil is contained in a separate tank and if the filler cap is removed the returning oil can be seen issuing from the stand-pipe. If there is no oil flow from the stand-pipe, stop the engine immediately, and investigate the cause. If, however, the oil tank has just been drained and refilled, and filters cleaned, there may be some delay before the oil is seen returning to the tank.

In order to keep the crankcase sump clear of oil—hence the term "dry-sump"—the scavenge portion of the pump must have a larger capacity than the supply side, and therefore, as the pump cannot return more oil than is supplied, the returning oil will contain a certain amount of air, showing itself in the form of bubbles—a normal condition for this lubrication system. The size of the escape hole in the stand-pipe is such that slight pressure is generated in the return pipe, and in the case of the O.H.V. models, some of the returning oil is tapped off at a union adjacent to the tank and fed to the rocker mechanism, afterwards draining down the push-rod tunnel to the crankcase sump. This oil feed was not fitted to the earlier C11G models, but as it was found that in certain circumstances there was a tendency for the rockers to run dry, it was added at engine No. BC11G-25901, and became standard thereafter on the C12 and all O.H.V. engines. Owners of C11G machines with engine numbers prior to the one given, can readily convert their lubrication system to the later designs, the extra pipe and fittings being obtainable through a B.S.A. dealer.

The only external oil pipes are those to and from the tank, and their connexions must always be kept tight.

C10L, C11G, C12 Models. The pipe lines from the tank and from the crankcase are joined together by synthetic rubber sleeves, which must be replaced if there is any doubt as to their efficiency. In the case of the return oil pipe, a defective sleeve will be indicated by oil-leakage, because of the slight pressure in the pipe, but a faulty supply-pipe sleeve is more difficult to detect. As the delivery portion of the oil pump is drawing oil from the tank, it can also draw in air past a defective sleeve, causing a partial failure of the oil supply to the engine. This will show itself by causing a considerably reduced flow of oil back to the tank, which can be detected after removing the oil tank filler cap while the engine is running. If it is found necessary to replace the sleeves, the ends of the pipes should be set carefully in line, to avoid internal chafing of the sleeves and eventual failure.

250 STAR MODELS. The flexible pipes are of armoured synthetic rubber, attached to short steel union pipes at both crankcase and oil tank. The ferrules on the ends of the rubber pipes are essential, and ensure a tight

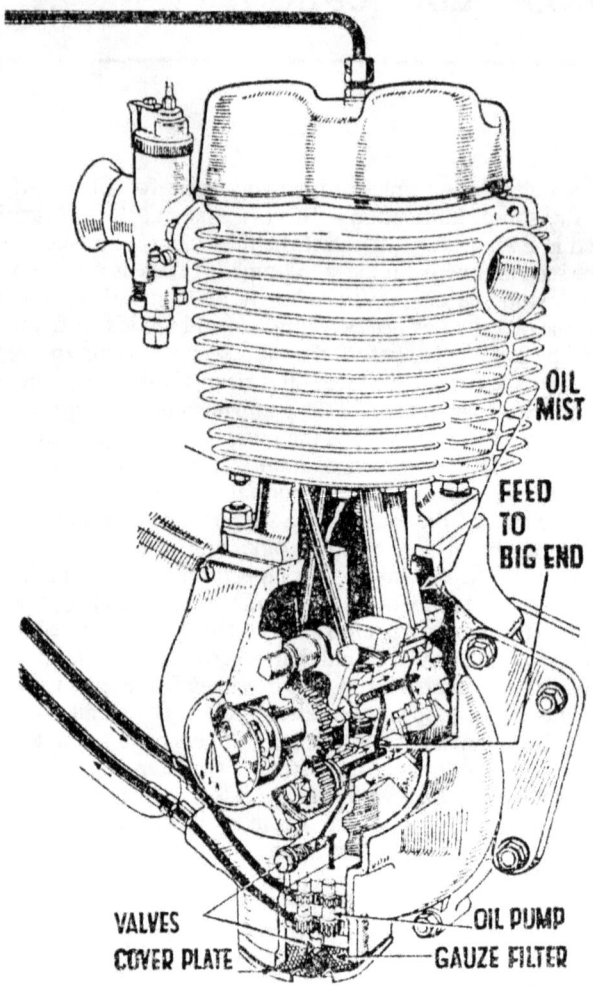

FIG. 1. THE LUBRICATION SYSTEM ON B.S.A. 250 c.c. C11G AND C12 ENGINES

The C10L engine is similar except for the oil feed to the rockers.

fit between the two pipes. They must always be replaced if the pipes have been disconnected.

BARRACUDA AND STARFIRE MODELS. These, together with later 250 Stars (C15G engines), utilized plain rubber pipes retained by clips. When replacing these pipes it is vital that they cross over before being attached to their engine-union pipes. Later models used pipes of differing bores to ensure correct assembly.

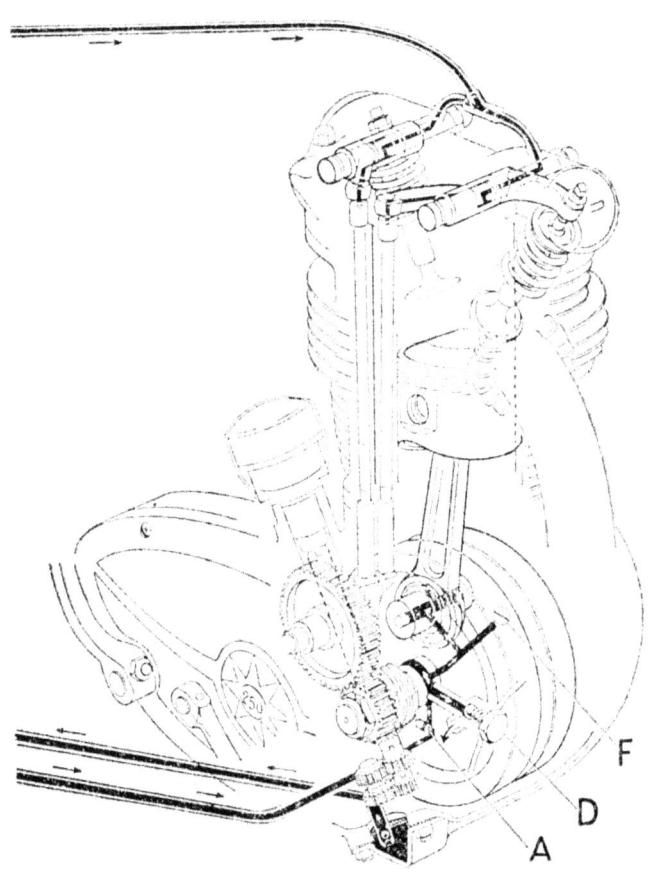

FIG. 2. THE LUBRICATION SYSTEM ON THE B.S.A. 250 c.c. STAR
The Star Model is C15 and there are the Sport Star Model C15SS, a Trials Star Model C15T, a Scrambles Model C15S, and the Sportsman. The car-type "distributor" shown above was superseded by a crankcase-mounted contact-breaker after 1964.

In a dry-sump lubrication system, the oil being in constant circulation, there is a gradual deterioration of its lubricating properties. This is due to the oil being used over and over again, and to the impurities it collects from the products of combustion.

For this reason the oil slowly becomes black in appearance, and should be changed at regular intervals in order to avoid undue wear of the moving parts. This is even more necessary in these days of high-detergency engine oils, which carry the impurities in suspension. Not only must the oil be changed, but the filters in the system must be cleaned at the same time, and the ball-valves kept in proper working order. Provided that these simple tasks are undertaken at intervals of, say, 2,000 miles, the lubrication system will function satisfactorily without further attention other than replenishment of the oil tank as required.

RECOMMENDED OILS AND GREASES (All Models)

Brand	Castrol	Mobil	Shell	B.P. Energol	Texaco	Esso
Engine oil	GTX	Super	Super 100	Visco-static 20W/50	Havoline 20W/50	Uniflo
Gearbox oil	Hypoy 90EP	Mobilube GX90	Spirax 90EP	Gear oil 90EP	Multi-gear 90EP	Gear oil 90EP
Front forks, chain-case oil	Castrolite	Super	Super 101	Visco-static 10W/40	Havoline 10W/30	Motor oil 10W/30
Grease	Castrol-ease LM	Mobil-grease MP, or Special	Retinax A	Ener-grease L2	Marfak All-purpose	Multi-purpose H

The Oil Pump. Because of the fine limits to which the pump is made, it is strongly recommended that it is not dismantled, unless it is *proved* to be at fault, when it is essential for a complete new pump to be obtained, as these are specially tested for efficiency at the Works, a procedure which the private owner cannot carry out.

For the final year of its production (1970), an improved oil pump was fitted to the Starfire. This pump is interchangeable *as a complete unit* with the pump fitted to earlier Starfire and Barracuda models.

Draining the Oil Tank. It will be appreciated that oil flows much more easily when warm than when cold, so that the operation of draining the tank will be simplified if it is carried out immediately after a run, when the oil has reached its normal working temperature.

C10L, C11G AND C12 MODELS. On all these machines the oil tank is fitted with a drain plug accessible from the offside, and it is, therefore, possible (but not desirable) to drain the tank without disturbing the filter. Replace the drain plug securely and re-fill with 4 pints of the correct grade of engine oil. (*See* "Recommended Engine Oils," above.)

250 STAR MODELS. When it becomes necessary to drain the oil tank, it is also advisable to remove and clean the filter. For this reason, a separate drain plug is considered to be superfluous, and on these models the drain plug and filter are combined. First disconnect the flexible oil pipe at its

union with the filter immediately below the tank, and then unscrew the filter body carrying with it the gauze sleeve.

BARRACUDA AND STARFIRE MODELS. It is unnecessary to disconnect the oil pipe on these models; merely unscrew the filter for draining purposes leaving the banjo union still connected to the pipe.

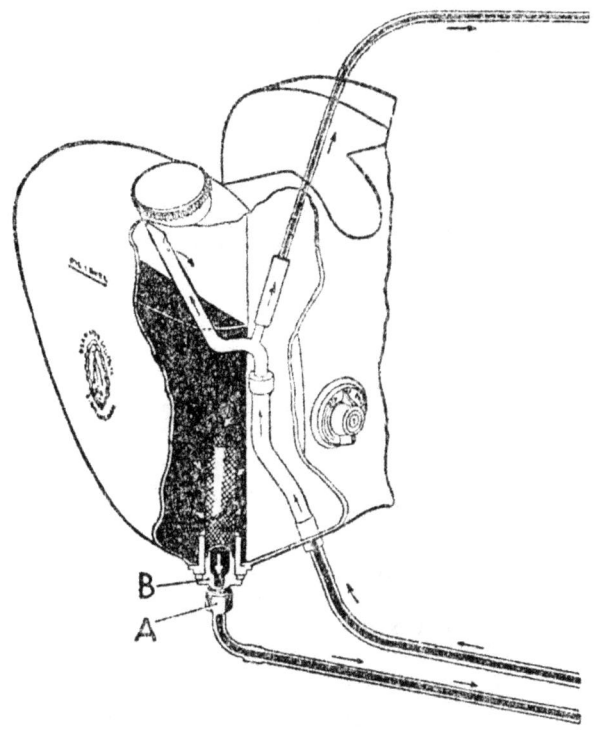

FIG. 3. A TYPICAL OIL TANK ASSEMBLY
The position and fixing of the oil filter varies with different models.

ALL MODELS. It is not advisable to use paraffin or similar liquids for flushing out the interior of the tank, because of the possibility that some may become trapped in the tank and dilute the new oil. Replace the filter securely and re-fill the tank with 4 pints of the correct grade of engine oil. (*See* "Recommended Engine Oils," page 4.)

Oil Tank Breather. It has been explained earlier that oil returning to the tank contains air and provision has to be made for its release. In the case of the C10L, C11G and C12 models, this takes the form of a built-in pipe, its upper end well above the oil level, and its lower end protruding from below the tank. Any restriction in this pipe will cause the pressure in the tank to rise and may result in leakage of oil at the filler cap. In this event, insert a piece of stiff wire into the pipe at its lower end, and push upwards until it is certain that the pipe is clear. A variation of this scheme is used on the 250 Star, Barracuda and Starfire machines. A very short breather pipe protrudes from either the back or the top of the tank, whence a flexible tube leads any escaping oil mist on to the rear chain. The amount of lubricant reaching the chain will be very small, and should not be regarded as an excuse for failing to carry out normal chain lubrication. (*See* page 9.)

Cleaning the Filters. On the C10L and C11G models of 1954-55, the filter body served a dual purpose and retained the banjo union of the oil supply pipe, but for the 1956-57 models of the C10L, and the 1956-57-58 C12 machines, the filter was entirely independent, and could be unscrewed from the lower offside of the tank without disturbing the supply pipe connexion. The 250 Star filters are constructed differently from any of the foregoing. With these models, the supply pipe screws onto the base of the filter, and only after removal of the pipe can the filter itself be unscrewed. The filter can be unscrewed independently on the Barracuda and Starfire models, leaving the union attached to the supply pipe. (*See* "Draining the Oil Tank," page 4.)

A second filter is carried below the crankcase and oil passes through the gauze before reaching the sump. The latter is retained by four nuts, and the gauze is at the centre of a "sandwich" on each side of which is an oil-proof gasket for the prevention of leakages. On 250 Star, Barracuda and Starfire models the gauze filter is attached to the sump plate and is withdrawn with it.

On these models, after replacing the sump plate, add about half a pint of engine oil into the crankcase (via the small plug hole on the left side of the case, at the front) to ensure immediate lubrication of all internal parts and to assist in priming the oil pump. Operate the starter pedal about thirty times (with the ignition switched off), until oil issues from the return pipe in the tank. The lubrication system is now in normal working order.

Non-Transfer Valves. To prevent any likelihood of oil transfer, two ball valves are fitted in the oilways. One of these is in the pump suction pipe and is visible when the crankcase sump plate is removed for the purpose of cleaning the filter. Examine the ball and make sure it is seating properly. If it is stuck to its seating, it will be impossible for the oil to return to the tank and a piece of steel wire should be inserted into the valve orifice to free the ball. A second ball valve is fitted in the oilway between the delivery pump and the big-end. Oil transfer is an unusual occurrence, but should this arise on any of the C10L, C11G or C12 engines, first thoroughly clean the ball and its seat, and if this is not effective replace the ball on its seat and give it a sharp tap with a light hammer and brass drift to ensure a good seating. Oil transfer had, in fact, become so rare, that when the newly designed 250 Star was introduced, this particular ball valve was fitted on the inside of the crankcase, and therefore does not require attention until the engine receives a complete overhaul. This method has been retained on the Barracuda and Starfire engines.

By-pass Valve. For the first time on a B.S.A. single-cylinder engine, a plain bearing was used in the big-end of the 250 Star up to 1965 and in order to avoid excessive build-up of pressure within the lubrication system, a special valve is fitted (*see* D, Fig. 2), which opens when a predetermined pressure has been reached, and allows the surplus oil to return to the crankcase sump. On later models, the surplus oil is diverted to lubricate the distributor driving gears on its way to the sump. This valve rarely gives trouble as it is continuously washed with oil under pressure. It should not need attention until the engine is dismantled for overhaul.

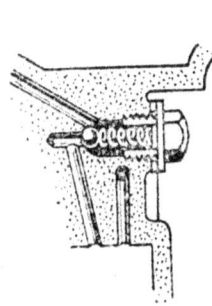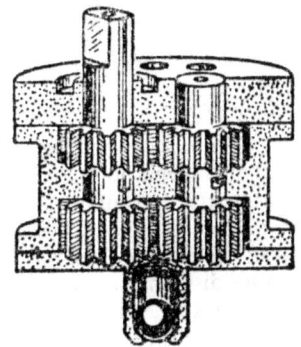

Fig. 4. (*left*) Spring-loaded Non-return Ball Valve in the Crankcase (C10L, C11G, C12)
(*right*) Non-return Ball Valve in the Base of the Gear-type Oil Pump

On engines of Scramblers type models numbered C15S–2449 to 2588 and from 3001, together with "Trials" engines from number C15T–1320, the plain big-end is replaced by a roller-bearing, without effecting the use of the by-pass valve. A roller bearing big-end was also introduced on the 250 Star and sports models at the commencement of the 1965 season and continued until production ceased in 1967. Barracuda and Starfire models have thin-wall plain big-end bearings and use a similar by-pass valve as shown at D, Fig. 2, except for the 1970 season, when the valve was designed as a detachable, self-contained unit, incorporating a spring-loaded plunger. As with the earlier types, this valve does not need attention until the engine is dismantled for overhaul.

Oil Pressure Switch. Introduced on 1970 Starfire models, this switch is mounted on the crankcase above the by-pass valve, D, Fig. 2. It is tapped into the duct between the oil pump and big-end, and when the pressure in the lubricating system is dangerously low, a red warning light is illuminated on top of the headlamp. **If this warning light appears at any engine speed other than "tick-over", or when first switching on the ignition (i.e. stationary engine), stop the engine immediately and investigate the cause,** otherwise serious damage may ensue.

THE MOTOR-CYCLE PARTS

Primary Chaincase. There must always be sufficient oil within the primary chaincase, not only for the obvious reason that it is necessary for the proper lubrication of the chain, but also to assist in dissipating the heat generated by a high-speed chain. On the other hand, the friction material used in the clutch (which is also in the chaincase) is such that whilst it can function satisfactorily when covered with a light film of oil, it is not designed to operate under conditions where it is flooded with oil. Too little oil, therefore, will not lubricate the chain properly; too much oil may cause the clutch to slip.

C10L, C11G AND C12 MODELS. The chaincase on these models is of pressed-steel, with a special sealing gasket between the two halves, in order to make an oil-tight joint. The outer half of the case carries the filler and level plugs, and a drain plug is fitted in the inner half, which also carries a sliding oil-seal to allow for movement of the gearbox for the purpose of adjusting the primary chain. Attention to any leakage at this point will necessitate dismantling the clutch as described on page 46. The oil level requires checking, and replenishment carried out, if required, at intervals of approximately 1,000 miles.

250 STAR, BARRACUDA AND STARFIRE MODELS. The primary chaincase on these models is in cast aluminium, the design being such that two of the screws in the lower part of the perimeter act as level and drain screws respectively. Both are identified by being coloured red, and the front one (which is also the higher of the two) determines the oil level. An inspection cap is provided on the chaincase for adjustment of the clutch, and this serves as the filler plug. A small, non-adjustable metered feed from the back of the case supplies a little lubricant to the rear chain, so that the level in the chaincase can be expected to fall steadily. For this reason, the oil level should be examined every 500 miles, replenishment with oil being made as required (*see* page 4).

When this is done, the machine should be standing upright and on level ground. Remove the level plug or screw, as the case may be, followed by the filler plug, and add oil until it flows from the level hole. Allow any surplus to drain off before replacing the plug or screw.

STARFIRE (1970 MODELS ONLY). A special boss cast on the chaincase cover, houses the oil level screw and hence is independent of the securing screws at the rim of the case. In addition, the oil feed to the rear chain is specified for certain countries only (which include the United Kingdom, but not U.S.A.)

B.S.A. LUBRICATION

The Gearbox. Normally, the gearbox calls for little maintenance, apart from ensuring that the correct oil level is maintained. This is important because of the use of plain bearings used on one or other of the shafts. The box should be drained and re-filled to the correct level with oil every 2,000 miles (*see* page 4), and this task is best undertaken when the gearbox is warm after a run.

C10L, C11G AND C12 MODELS. The gearboxes on these machines are fitted with level plugs located in all cases at the rear of the box (*see* Fig. 20). The filler cap is on the outer cover and is either a screwed cap or, in the case of the C11G four-speed box, an oval inspection cap retained by two screws. A drain plug (G, Fig. 21) is also fitted to all these gearboxes.

250 STAR MODELS. Level and drain plugs are combined as a unit. The level is determined by means of a stand-pipe attached to the drain plug and protrudes vertically into the box. To check the level, remove the small screw (K, Fig. 40), from the centre of the drain plug and if necessary remove the filler cap (T) and add gear oil (*see* page 4). When draining, it will be noted that the stand-pipe is withdrawn with the drain plug (S).

It was eventually found necessary to raise the oil level, so that for engines prior to No. C15–25462 and C15S–2181, the procedure already given should be carried out first, and then, after the level plug has been replaced, add a further quarter-of-a-pint of oil. For gearboxes on machines produced after the engine numbers given had been reached, the oil level was re-adjusted by a design modification and it is unnecessary to add an extra quantity of oil.

BARRACUDA AND STARFIRE MODELS (1967). The oil level is determined by a stand pipe as shown in Fig. 40.

STARFIRE MODELS (1968–70). The filler plug carries a dipstick giving the oil level.

Front Forks. (C10L (1954–5 ONLY).) The forks on these models are not of the hydraulic type and there is no method of adjustment. The only attention required is regular lubrication of the fork sliding members by means of grease nipples in the lower part of the fork leg. Also remove the gaiters and clean and grease the sliding members at intervals of 3,000 miles.

ALL OTHER MODELS. The primary purpose of the oil contained within each of the fork legs is not for lubrication purposes (although it also serves this purpose), but as a damping medium for the telescopic action of the fork. Attention to the forks is therefore dealt with under the heading "Steering and Suspension," page 91.

Rear Chain. It is advisable to use the oil can at weekly intervals. Little and often is the best policy, as too liberal an amount of oil may result in an oil-spattered machine. At intervals of about 2,000 miles, it is beneficial for the chain to be taken off and washed thoroughly in paraffin to remove all dirt and grease. Immerse it in a tray of warmed graphited grease, allow to cool and wipe off surplus grease. When replacing the chain, make sure that the "hairpin" spring clip on the connecting link has its closed end pointing in the direction of travel of the chain. This is important because it guards against the chain becoming accidentally disconnected.

ON 250 STAR, BARRACUDA AND STARFIRE MODELS. The chain is automatically lubricated from the primary chaincase via a metered feed, *see* page 8, but it is still advisable to treat the chain to a grease bath at intervals as described on page 9.

Grease-gun and Oil-can Lubrication. The points requiring an application of the grease gun will be obvious on inspection, and other moving parts are lubricated by oil.

There are, however, several items worthy of special mention. Hubs on the C10L and C11G machines should be greased at 1,000-mile intervals. Two or three strokes of the gun is sufficient at any one time otherwise grease may reach the brakes. On the C12, 250 Star, Barracuda and Starfire models, ball journal bearings are fitted to the hubs and packed with grease on assembly. No further attention is required until such time as the hubs are dismantled.

The brake cams on the C10L, C11G and C12 machines are lubricated with oil, after moving aside a spring clip. One or two spots only are required. Similarly, one stroke of the grease gun is all that is required on the 250 Star brake cams. In both cases, if overdone, the lubricant may find its way on to the brake linings.

The speedometer of C10L and C11G machines having three-speed gearboxes, is driven from the rear hub by means of a worm-drive, which should receive two or three strokes of the gun every 2,000 miles.

The "swinging arm" pivot bearings are of bonded rubber on model C12 and require no lubrication, but on the 250 Star machines, regular greasing is required at not more than 1,000-mile intervals. On the competition versions of this model, it is preferable to grease this pivot before every event. Bonded rubber pivot bearings were re-introduced on the Barracuda and Starfire models and lubrication is unnecessary.

The majority of machines are fitted with dual seats, but some C10L and C11G models were supplied with saddles, in which case the nose bolt requires weekly greasing.

In order to prevent the hand controls from becoming stiff in action the exposed cable ends should be oiled every week, together with all control-rod joints. As an additional aid to smooth operation of the clutch, the cable on 1969–70 Starfires is fitted with a grease nipple. Apply grease at intervals of 2,000 miles.

Also lubricate such items as the brake pedal shaft, rear chain and central stand.

2 General Maintenance

A LITTLE *regular servicing* will pay handsome dividends, and make even slower the slow process of wear and tear, which is inevitable in the moving parts. Such maintenance will help to keep the engine at concert pitch, so that it will respond to the twist-grip with its full power output, and *regular attention* to other working parts will ensure sweetly running transmission, quiet gear changes, accurate steering and so on.

Valve Clearances. The valves are operated by cams, acting through tappets, direct onto the valve stems of S.V. engines, or, in the case of O.H.V engines, through a train of parts comprising tappets, push-rods and overhead rockers. A definite clearance between the valve stem and tappet, or valve stem and rocker, according to engine type, is essential.

With a machine which has covered an appreciable mileage, a pocket may have been worn in the tappet head (S.V.) or valve stem, in which case it will be impossible to measure the gap satisfactorily. Provided that the depression is not too deep, the surface can be ground flat again, but otherwise the component concerned should be replaced.

The valve clearances are measured by means of "feeler gauges." The clearances must be set in accordance with the figures given in Table I, and always with the engine cold.

TABLE I. VALVE CLEARANCES

Valve	C10L	C11G and C12	250 Star, SS.80, Barracuda and Starfire	250 Star Scrambler	250 Star Trials
Inlet Closed	0·004 in. before eng. 3562 0·012 in. from eng. 3562	0·003 in. before eng. 10438 0·010 in. from eng. 10438	0·008	0·004 in. before eng. 3001 0·008 in. from eng. 3001	0·004 in. before eng. 1251 0·008 in. from eng. 1251
Exhaust Closed	0·006 in. before eng. 3562 0·015 in. from eng. 3562	0·003 in. before eng. 10438 0·012 in. from eng. 10438	0·010	0·004 in. before eng. 3001 0·010 in. from eng. 3001	0·004 in. before eng. 1251 0·010 in. from eng. 1251

Before checking the clearances, take out the sparking plug, which will enable the engine to be rotated much more easily by hand pressure on the kickstarter, and then carry out the checking or adjustment in accordance with the following procedure. Rotate the engine until the inlet valve has just closed (when the tappet (S.V.) or push-rod (O.H.V.) is just free enough to rotate), and adjust the exhaust valve clearance. Then rotate the engine again until the exhaust valve clearance is just taken up, but before the valve actually starts to lift, and adjust the inlet valve clearance.

C10L ENGINE. Take off the tappet cover at the base of the cylinder barrel, thus exposing both tappets. Apply a spanner to the tappet head A (Fig. 5), and a second one to the locknut B, which must be slackened off.

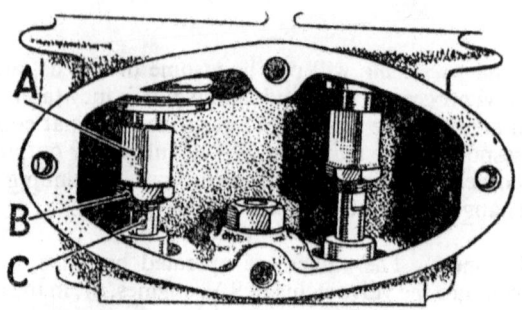

FIG. 5. TAPPET ADJUSTMENT ON S.V. MODEL C10L

Then hold the tappet stem with a spanner on the flats at C, and adjust the head up or down until the space between the valve stem and tappet head is just sufficient for the feeler gauge to enter. Now tighten the locknut firmly against the head, and check the clearance again to make sure that it did not alter when tightening the nut. Examine the cover gasket which must be in a sound condition in order to prevent oil leaks and replace carefully. Tighten the cover firmly.

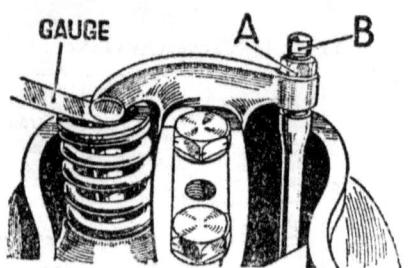

FIG. 6. VALVE CLEARANCE ADJUSTMENT ON O.H.V. MODELS C11G AND C12

C11G AND C12 ENGINES. Removal of the rocker cover on top of the cylinder head gives access to the rockers and their adjusting screws (*see* Fig. 6.) Hold the adjusting screw B stationary by means of a spanner applied to the flats, and with a second spanner, release locknut A. Rotate the screw up or down until there is just sufficient space between the rocker

GENERAL MAINTENANCE

arm and valve stem for the feeler gauge to enter, and re-tighten the locknut against the rocker arm. Check the clearance before replacing the cover and the gasket. Should the gasket be damaged it should be renewed.

250 STAR ENGINES. Adjustment of the valve clearances is carried out in a similar manner to that described for the C12 engine, except that the feeler gauge is fitted between the adjusting screw and the valve stem. (*See* Fig. 7.) A separate inspection cap is provided for each adjuster.

BARRACUDA AND STARFIRE ENGINES. Remove the inspection caps above both rocker arms. Eccentric spindles are used for adjustment purposes

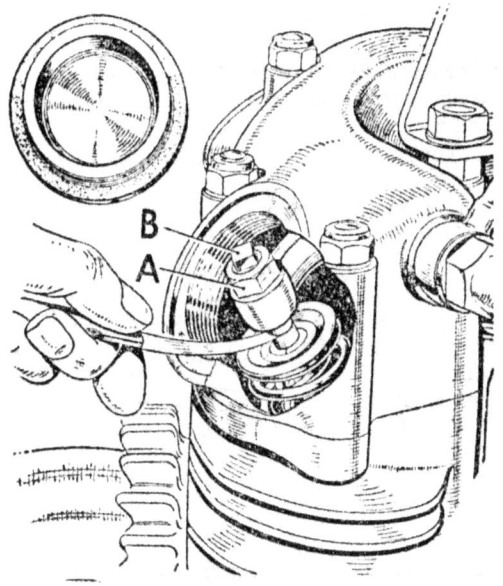

FIG. 7. VALVE CLEARANCE ADJUSTMENT ON ALL O.H.V. 250 STAR MODELS

and the valve clearances can be modified by rotation of the spindles as follows.

Remove the cover plate from the offside of the rocker-box to expose the slotted ends of the spindles (*see* Fig. 8) and slacken the lock-nuts on their opposite ends. Commence the setting operation with the spindles in what may be termed the "neutral" position (i.e. with the small flats at the inner edges and disposed vertically as shown in Fig. 8) rotate the exhaust spindle in an *anti-clockwise* direction and the inlet spindle in a *clockwise* direction* until the valve clearances comply with those given in Table I. Tighten the spindle lock-nuts and again check the clearances.

* On engines prior to engine No. C25-2050 (1967) the rocker spindles must be rotated in the opposite direction to that stated above.

If during the adjustment it is found that one of the spindles will no longer rotate in a forward (clockwise) direction, unscrew it one complete turn and recommence adjustment. Make sure that the cover-plate gasket is intact before replacement, otherwise it will not be oiltight.

The Exhaust-Valve Lifter. This is a device fitted to the Barracuda and Starfire engines as an aid to starting. Adjust the cable length to give ample clearance between the rocker arm and the lifter spindle. This is indicated by appreciable free movement of the handlebar lever before there is contact between the rocker and spindle, when the lever becomes stiff to operate. This control is *not* fitted to 1969–70 Starfires.

The Contact-breaker. Although the contact-breaker can be considered to be part of the electrical system, the adjustment of the contact points gap is described here, as it is a preliminary operation to that of checking the ignition timing. The moving arm, carrying one of the points, is subject to

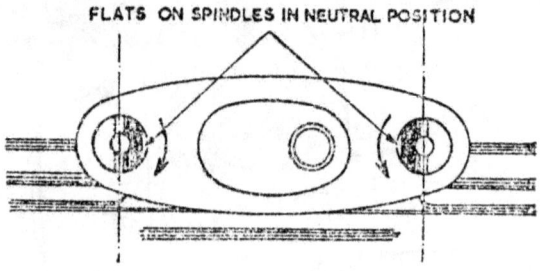

Fig. 8. Valve Clearance Adjustment on Barracuda and Starfire Engines

slight wear of its pad which bears on the cam (especially if the latter has not received its proper lubrication), and also to possible erosion of the points themselves. The points gap, therefore, should be checked at intervals of about 3,000 miles, and maintained at the correct setting.

Remove the sparking plug to enable the engine to be rotated easily by hand operation of the kickstarter, and turn it until the points gap B (Figs. 9, 10 and 11), and similar gap indicated in Figs. 12 and 13, is at its maximum. Check with feeler gauges and adjust as required to 0·015 in.

C10L Engine. The contact-breaker unit is mounted on the timing cover and enclosed by cap A (Fig. 9). The cap is retained by two screws and after its removal together with the sealing gasket, the unit is exposed. To adjust the points slacken the upper screw D (the pivot), and rotate the lower screw (the eccentric), so moving the fixed contact mounted on its adjustable plate. Re-tighten the pivot screw securely.

C11G and C12 Engines. Access to the contact-breaker points is obtained in the same way as for the C10L engine, and adjustment of the points differs only slightly. Slacken the two screws D (Fig. 10), one of

GENERAL MAINTENANCE

which acts as the pivot pin for the adjustable plate carrying the fixed contact. The other screw is for locking purposes, and operates in a slot in the same plate. When the gap is correct, re-tighten both screws securely.

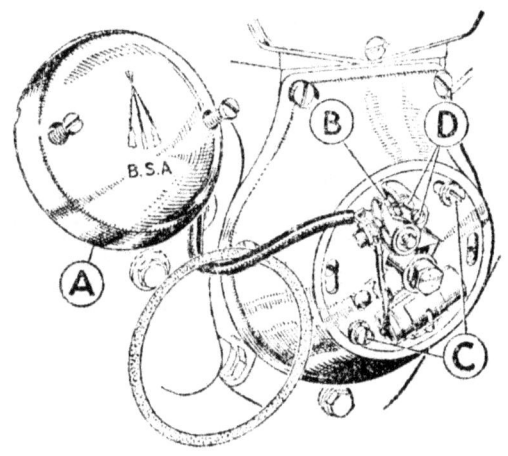

FIG. 9. CONTACT-BREAKER ASSEMBLY ON S.V. MODEL C10L

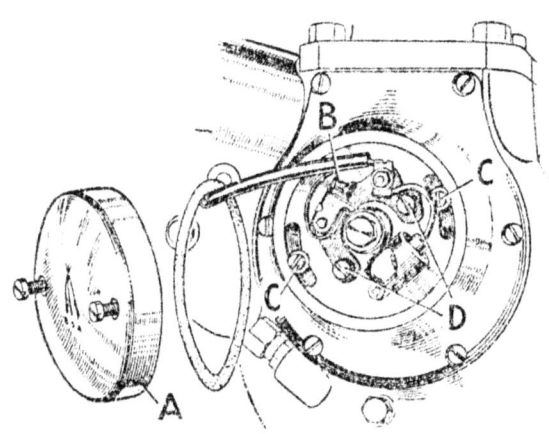

FIG. 10. CONTACT-BREAKER ASSEMBLY ON O.H.V. MODELS C11G AND C12

250 STAR ENGINES. The contact-breaker, together with its associated auto-advance mechanism, is in a self-contained unit, mounted above the crankcase behind the cylinder. Move aside the spring clip (or central screw on later models), and take off cover A (Fig. 11). The fixed contact point is attached to a plate mounted at right angles to the moving contact,

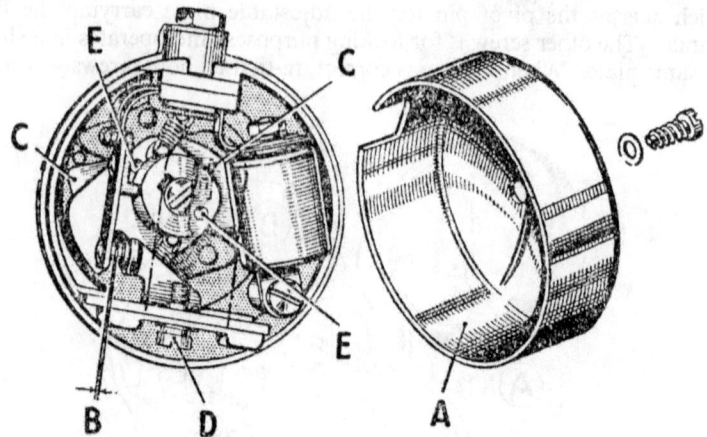

FIG. 11. CONTACT-BREAKER ASSEMBLY AND AUTO-ADVANCE UNIT ON THE O.H.V. 250 STAR MODEL PRIOR TO THE 1965 SEASON

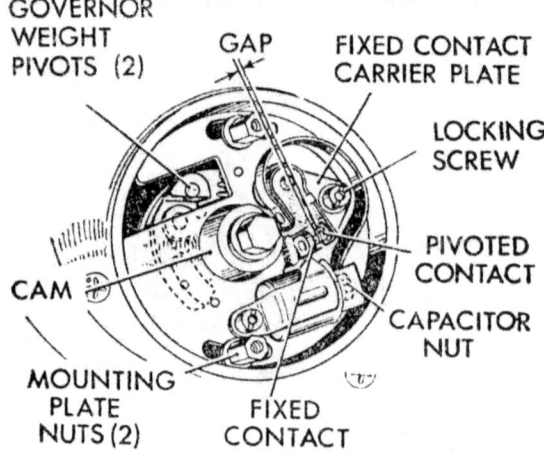

FIG. 12. CONTACT-BREAKER ASSEMBLY AND AUTO-ADVANCE UNIT ON 250 STARS MANUFACTURED AFTER 1964 AND UP TO 1967 (INCLUDING BARRACUDA AND STARFIRE)

and if adjustment is required, slacken screw D, move the plate until adjustment is correct, then re-tighten the screw securely.

For the 1965 season the car-type contact-breaker unit was discontinued, being replaced by a unit mounted in the timing side of the crankcase and driven off the camshaft.

GENERAL MAINTENANCE

The contact points gap is adjusted by first slackening the locking screw (Fig. 12) which secures the plate carrying the fixed contact. Adjust the plate until the gap is correct. Re-tighten the screw and check the adjustment.

BARRACUDA AND STARFIRE ENGINES (1967). The contact-breaker unit was the same as fitted to the 250 Star from 1965 onwards and Fig. 12 applies to these models.

STARFIRE ENGINES (1968–70). A new design of contact-breaker employing eccentric pin-adjusters was introduced for the 1968 season (*see* Fig. 13) making accurate adjustment extremely simple. It is only necessary to slacken the fixing screw D and, by means of the eccentric pin E, adjust the

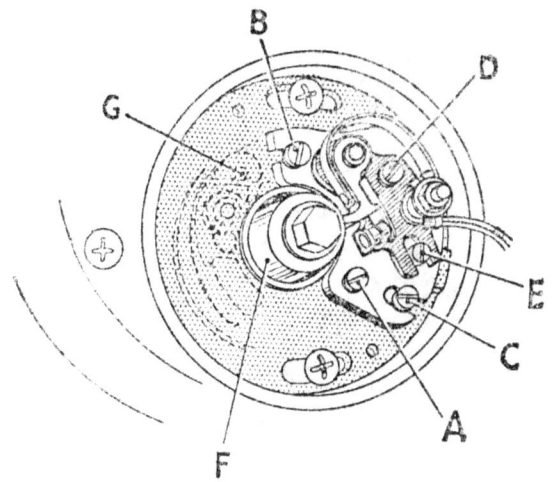

FIG. 13. THE CONTACT-BREAKER ASSEMBLY AND AUTO-ADVANCE UNIT (1968 STARFIRE ENGINES)

plate which carries the fixed-contact point, until the gap is correct. Re-tighten screw D firmly and check the adjustment.

Automatic Advance Mechanism. The contact points are opened and closed by means of a cam on the driving spindle, and the relationship of the cam with the spindle is controlled by means of a centrifugally operated governor, located immediately below the contact-breaker unit. When the engine is stationary, the governor springs draw the bob-weights to their inner position, where the timing is fully retarded and this is the normal position for checking the setting. As the engine speed increases, the bob-weights move outwards under the influence of centrifugal force, so progressively advancing the ignition timing, until it is fully advanced at normal road speeds.

The bob-weights C (Fig. 11), and B (Fig. 14), must move freely, and this should be tested by turning the cam to the advanced position, when the weights will be fully extended outwards. If the cam is then released, the springs should withdraw the weights to the inner, or retarded, position. If the weights are seized in the retarded position, performance will be poor, the engine will overheat, and eventually the exhaust valve will require renewal. Lubricate the bob-weight bearings with a spot or two of oil— no more—as over-lubrication may cause oil to find its way on to the contact points, making starting difficult.

C10L, C11G and C12. To expose the advance and retard mechanism remove the two screws C (Figs. 9 and 10), and detach the contact-breaker back plate complete with the unit. Models C11G and C12 are fitted with

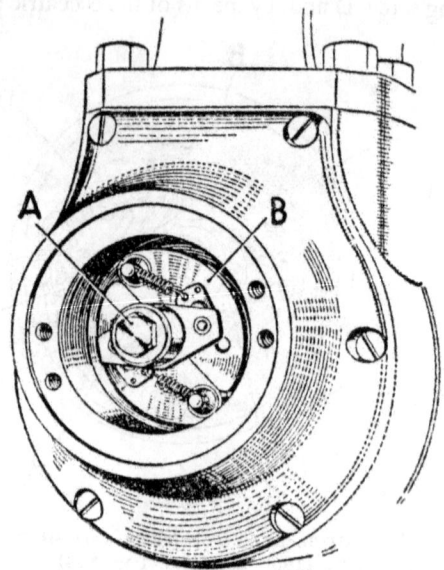

Fig. 14. Advance and Retard Mechanism on the S V. Model C10L and O.H.V. Models C11G and C12

Lucas equipment and experience with the C11G engine showed that improved advance and retard operation could be obtained by a change of bob-weight springs, the alteration becoming effective on engine No. C11G-34426 onwards.

250 Star Engines. When cap A (Fig. 11) is removed, the governor mechanism is directly visible, and it can receive attention without further dismantling. Similarly with the design shown in Fig. 12, the governor mechanism can be lubricated through the aperture in the mounting plate.

Starfire Engines (1968-70). The governor mechanism is not directly accessible for lubrication purposes and it will be necessary to remove the contact-breaker assembly.

The base plate carrying the unit is retained by two screws and removal of these allows the plate to be lifted off, complete with contact breaker.

GENERAL MAINTENANCE

Before removal, scribe a line across the plate and the housing, to enable the plate to be replaced in exactly the same position. Even so, it will then be advisable to check the ignition timing.

Ignition Timing. Whenever the contact-breaker gap has been re-adjusted the timing should be checked, because if the gap has been increased, then the timing will have been advanced slightly or, conversely, retarded if the gap has been closed. It follows, therefore, that whenever the ignition timing is to be checked, the contact-breaker gap must first be examined and re-set if required. Similarly, if the contact-breaker back plate on the C10L, C11G and C12 engines has been removed for inspection of the governor mechanism, the ignition timing should be checked following replacement of the plate.

Checking the timing is a straightforward operation, but one which requires care and accuracy in measurement of the settings. It will be necessary to turn the engine both forwards and backwards, and this is made easier if top gear is engaged, and the sparking plug taken out (O.H.V. engines), or the compression plug removed (S.V. engines).

Obtain a thin rod, such as a stout knitting needle, of such a length that it will not fall into the cylinder when the piston is at the bottom of its stroke, or foul the underside of the tank when the piston is at the top of its stroke. Insert the rod through the plug hole so that the piston position can be determined. Gently rotate the engine by hand pressure on the starter pedal, until the piston has reached the top of its compression stroke, when both valves will be closed. If either of them is open (and this can be detected through the plug hole on the O.H.V. engines or by checking the tappet position on the S.V. engine), the piston is on the wrong stroke, and the engine must be rotated through one more revolution, i.e. the piston must descend to the bottom of its stroke and then rise again to the top position.

Scribe a thin line on the rod level with some convenient point on the engine, then withdraw it and scribe a further mark above the original one, at a distance corresponding to the ignition timing given in Table II (*see* page 21). Re-insert the rod, rotate the engine backwards by turning the rear wheel until the piston has descended an inch or so, and then rotate the engine in a forward direction until the upper mark on the rod rises to the same point as did the original mark. This means that the piston is at its correct distance before the top of its stroke (i.e. before T.D.C.). It is essential to turn the engine backwards before bringing the piston to its proper position so as to take up any play in the timing gears. If this precaution be ignored, accurate ignition setting will not be possible.

With the piston in this position, the contact-breaker points should be just on the verge of opening. This is best determined by inserting a piece of very thin paper (such as a cigarette paper) between the points. They will be about to open when the paper can be withdrawn with a *gentle* pull.

On the C10L, C11G and C12 engines, the position of the contact points can be adjusted to give this condition by slackening the two screws C (Figs. 9 and 10), and moving the plate slightly one way or the other. With the 250 Star machines, it will be necessary to rotate the whole contact-breaker housing, which is free to move after its clip screw is slackened. This screw is the rearmost of the two at the top of the timing cover. (See also page 25.) When the setting is completed and all screws tightened again, repeat the whole procedure, to make doubly sure that nothing became disturbed while the operation was being carried out.

250 STAR TRIALS AND SCRAMBLES ENGINES. The "trials" and "scrambles" engines are equipped with what is termed the "Energy Transfer" ignition system, which calls for a different procedure when setting the ignition

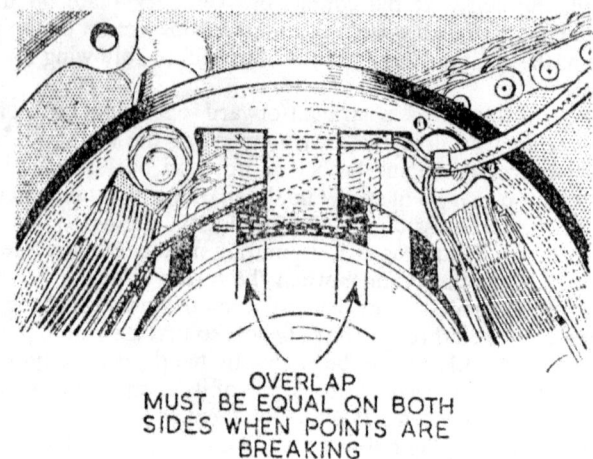

OVERLAP
MUST BE EQUAL ON BOTH
SIDES WHEN POINTS ARE
BREAKING

FIG. 15. IGNITION SETTING ON THE O.H.V. 250 STAR TRIALS AND SCRAMBLES MODELS

Not applicable after engine Nos. 3320 (scrambles) and 1530 (trials).

timing. This system of ignition is more sensitive to accurate timing than the normal coil ignition and as a preliminary to the main operation, the contact-breaker gap must be adjusted to 0·015 in.

Rotate the engine until the piston is at the top of its compression stroke, then rotate the engine backwards, until the piston has descended about 1 in. Turn the engine forwards again, to bring the rotor into the position shown in Fig. 15. It is essential for the engine to be turning in a forward direction when the position is obtained, and if it is turned too far, it must be reversed until the piston has descended by about 1 in., and the operation recommenced. In this position of the rotor, the contact-breaker points should be just about to open.

A mid-season change on the 250 Star engines (including the "trials" and "scrambles" models) introduced a new contact-breaker auto-advance unit, having a reduced range between full advance and full retard. This resulted in revised ignition timings, and engine numbers when this alteration became effective were 41600 (250 Star), 2585 (Sport Star), 3320 (Scrambles) and 1530 (Trials).

GENERAL MAINTENANCE

The method of checking or setting the ignition timing is as detailed previously, except that the piston is 0·007 in. before T.D.C. instead of the $\frac{1}{16}$ in. given in Table II. If any difficulty is experienced in measuring the new piston position it will simplify matters if an alternative method is used. With the aid of a degree plate the crankshaft can be set at 5 degrees before T.D.C. giving the above piston position.

A design change for the 1965 season introduced a new contact-breaker mechanism (Fig. 12). The ignition setting can be adjusted by first slackening the mounting-plate nuts and then moving the plate one way or the other, to give the required setting. For the 1968 Starfire setting, the

TABLE II. IGNITION SETTINGS
(Piston distance before T.D.C.)

C10L	C11G, C12	250 Star	Barracuda Starfire
$\frac{1}{32}$ in. on Full retard	T.D.C. before engine BC11G–34426 $\frac{3}{64}$ in. from engine BC11G–34426 Fully retarded	$\frac{1}{16}$ in. (0·062 in.) or 0·007 in. Fully retarded	
		$\frac{9}{32}$ in. (0·28 in.) Fully advanced (Models after 1964)	0·342 in. Fully advanced

mounting plate is not disturbed but instead, the *contact-breaker* plate is adjusted. The required setting is obtained by first slackening the screws A and B (Fig. 13) when rotation of the eccentric pin C will move the whole assembly circumferentially.

Note that from 1965 the contact-breaker adjustment must be made with the auto-advance mechanism set in the fully advanced position (*see* Table II). This position can be obtained if the washer behind the central fixing bolt is temporarily replaced by another, having a hole a little larger than the cam bearing. Rotate the cam until the governor weights are fully open and tighten the bolt, thus locking the cam in the fully advanced position. Remember to replace the old washer afterwards, otherwise the auto-advance mechanism will be inoperative.

If the contact-breaker has been completely freed from its driving spindle, either inadvertently or when the engine is being re-built, it should be replaced in the approximately correct position before re-adjusting as above, because the mounting plate gives limited adjustment only. The approximate position is with the piston at the top of the compression stroke and the contact points just opening. The unit locks onto a taper seat and the approximate position should be selected carefully before tightening the centre bolt. The method of checking the relationship between piston and contact-breaker points is as described previously but, for a fully advanced setting, the piston is 0·28 in. before T.D.C. or alternatively, if a degree plate is used, 33½ degrees. For the Barracuda and Starfire engines the corresponding figures are 0·342 in. before T.D.C. or, using a degree plate, 37°.

BARRACUDA AND STARFIRE ENGINES. The manual method of setting the ignition timing, described in the previous sections, requires great care to ensure accurate results, but on these two engines provision is made for an alternative method involving the use of a "Strobelite" which gives precise results.

Removal of the inspection cover at the front of the primary chaincase will reveal a pointer on the case and a marker line on the rotor. The engine must be run at a speed high enough to ensure that the ignition is *fully advanced* when, with the intermittent beam from the Strobelite projected on to the rotor, the latter will appear to become stationary and the marker line will be exactly opposite to the pointer if the timing is correct.

Any adjustment to obtain the above condition should be made as described on page 21. Note that the Strobelite must be coupled to an independent battery and must, of course, be connected in accordance with its maker's instructions.

The Sparking Plug. If the carburation is in correct adjustment, and the engine in good condition, the sparking plug points and the interior of the plug generally should remain clean. If the mixture is too rich (which should also be indicated in heavy petrol consumption), a soft sooty deposit forms on the points and interior of the plug. On the other hand, if a weak mixture has been used for some time, the points become white in appearance. If a fuel containing a heavy lead content is used, a greyish deposit may result. A hard, black deposit which has to be scraped off the plug body, is an indication of excess oil. This becomes burnt onto the plug and the remainder of the combustion chamber space, and is usually an indication that the piston rings and cylinder bore are in poor condition.

If any of these deposits remain undisturbed, the build-up of carbon inside the plug body may cause the plug to short internally, with a consequent adverse effect on engine performance.

The plug, which cannot be dismantled for cleaning purposes, should be cleaned and tested at intervals of 2,000 miles, on a sand-and-air blast unit, which is available at most garages. After cleaning, make certain that the interior of the plug is free from oil and abrasive, before replacing in the engine.

The correct gap for engines with coil ignition is 0·020 in.–0·025 in. and is measured by means of a feeler gauge inserted between the points. If any re-setting is required, the gap must always be corrected by bending the side or earthed electrode towards, or away from, the centre one. Never

GENERAL MAINTENANCE

attempt to bend the centre electrode, as this may damage the insulation, and lead to an ineffective plug.

Screw the plug in as far as possible by hand (especially necessary in the case of aluminium cylinder heads), using a box spanner for the final tightening.

Suitable Sparking Plugs. Champion sparking plugs recommended by B.S.A. Motor Cycles Ltd. are those specified in Table III. All have a 14 mm. thread size and all have a ¾ in. reach, except the Champion L7 which has a ½ in. reach.

All four of the sparking plug makes referred to in this chapter are of proved quality and reliability, and equally serviceable. All are non-detachable, requiring a garage "blast unit" for blasting out deposits and testing.

TABLE III

RECOMMENDED CHAMPION PLUGS

C10L	C11G, C12	250 Star	SS80, Sportsman	Scrambles, Barracuda, Starfire	Trials Models
N8	L7	N5	N4	N3	N5

Valve Timing. If it becomes essential to remove and replace the gears, it will be found that they are marked so that the teeth engage in their correct relationship with each other, and automatically give the correct valve timing (*see* Figs. 16 and 17). Access to the gears is a straightforward dismantling matter, but there is rather more work involved with the 250 Star engines than with the others, because of the unit construction of the engine and gearbox. Dismantling the timing case will also involve disturbing the ignition timing, and with all engines, once the valve timing has been set to its correct marks, it will be necessary to re-time the ignition in accordance with the instructions given on page 19.

C10L, C11G, C12 ENGINES. The camshaft gear drive is contained within the timing case on the offside of the crankcase, and lies behind the contact-breaker unit. First remove cover A (*see* Fig. 9), and then the contact-breaker back plate (*see* page 18). This will expose the auto-advance mechanism which is attached to the camshaft by the central bolt A (*see* Fig. 14), via a taper diameter and a locating peg. Unscrew the bolt, but as the spindle is still retained by the taper, it will be necessary to make a simple extractor. The requirements for this are, a piece of 3/16 in. rod 3½ in. long, and a 5/16 in., 26 t.p.i. bolt ⅜ in. long. Insert the rod into the hole, screw in the extractor bolt until it touches the end of the rod, when a sharp jerk on the spanner will free the spindle from the taper.

A mid-season change of design on the 1954 C10L and C11G engines introduced a modified central bolt, which also acted as an extractor. All C12 engines were fitted with this type of bolt.

The timing case is held by six screws and two dowels, and after its removal, the gasket, camshaft complete with gear, cam followers, etc., can be removed. Whatever the reason for dismantling to this stage, examine the cam followers, and if their contact faces at the camshaft are excessively worn, they should be replaced with a later type incorporating contact pads of a special material brazed in position. These are suitable for the O.H.V. models.

Two points must be specially watched, when reassembling. The first of these concerns the replacement of the timing cover. This carries an oil

FIG. 16. VALVE-TIMING MARKS FOR S.V. MODEL C10L AND O.H.V. MODELS C11G AND C12

seal which fits over the outer end of the camshaft, and prevents oil leakage from its bearing into the contact-breaker compartment. Great care must be exercised to make sure that the lip of the seal is not damaged in any way, and it must be replaced if there are any doubts as to its efficiency. The lip of the seal must be facing the inside of the engine. The second point is that the peg on the taper spindle must be lined up with the slot in the camshaft, before tightening the central bolt. The timing cover gasket must, of course, be in good condition to prevent oil leakage.

250 STAR ENGINES (PRE-1965). The timing gears are within the inner timing cover. First the outer cover must be removed and this requires prior removal of the exhaust system, gearchange pedal, and kickstarter pedal. The exhaust pipe, incidentally, is a push-fit in the cylinder head, and may require a sharp blow with a soft mallet to free it. The gearchange pedal is held on to its serrations by means of a clip bolt, and the footchange lever by a cotter pin, which must be driven out after removing the nut. The screws

GENERAL MAINTENANCE 25

round the edge of the cover necessitate the use of a special screwdriver for their removal as they have recessed heads. It should be noted that when the rearmost of the two screws at the top of the cover is taken out, the clip retaining the contact-breaker unit is freed and hence the contact-breaker itself is free to move, involving re-timing in due course.

The next step is to disconnect the clutch cable, which is simply a matter of depressing the lever, lifting the nipple out of its slot, and withdrawing the cable and its adaptor from the rear of the cover. The thrust plunger

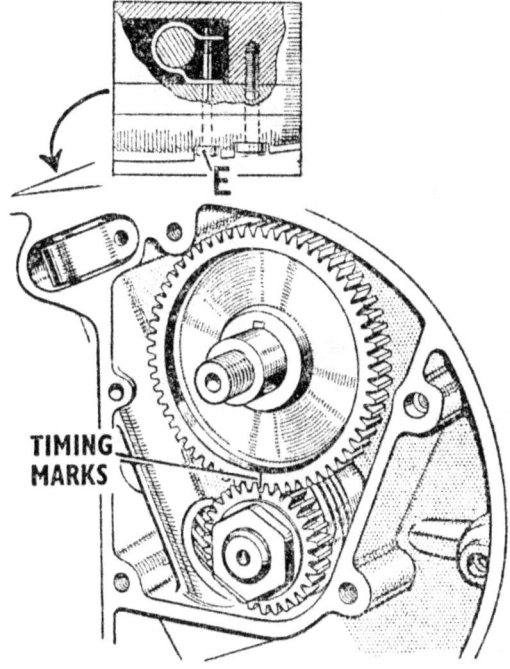

FIG. 17. VALVE-TIMING MARKS FOR THE O.H.V. STAR ENGINE

The distributor retaining clip and the screw *E*, do not apply to the Star engines produced after 1964, nor to the Barracuda and Starfire, but the timing marks are the same.

mounted on the lever carries a small ball, which can readily fall out and be lost. It is advisable to remove the ball and put it on one side ready for re-assembly, when a dab of grease will be found useful for holding it in position. After 1964, the clutch-control lever is above the timing case and it is simply a matter of slackening off all the adjustment at the handle-bar lever and withdrawing the cable nipple from the control. The kickstarter spring is operated by means of a tongued disc, which rotates with the starter spindle and is keyed to it by means of two parallel flat surfaces. Prise the disc off the spindle with the aid of a screwdriver or similar tool, so that both spring and disc become free and can be removed. The inner end of the spring is hooked over the end of the special screw, which should not be taken out unless it is desired to remove the kickstarter stop plate on the inner face of the cover.

Attention can now be given to the small plate just behind the gearchange spindle. This covers the pivot for the camplate, which operates the selector forks within the gearbox, and the camplate itself must remain inside the box when the inner cover is taken away. Remove the cover

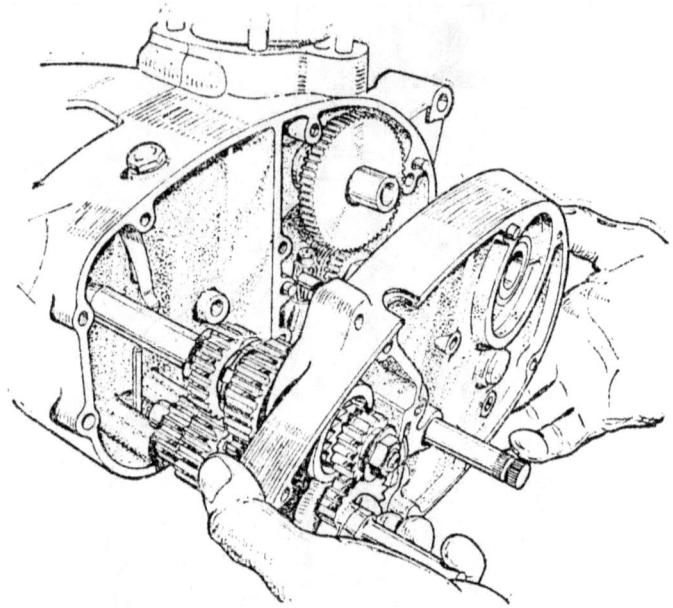

Fig. 18. Removing the Inner Timing Cover
Applies to recent Barracuda, Starfire models, and to the 1967 250 Star.

plate, withdraw the split-pin which retains the pivot in position, and take out the latter rearwards. There now remains the camshaft nut, which is locked by means of a tab washer. This must first be straightened before the nut can be unscrewed, and the thrust washer and locating peg removed.

The inner cover is attached to the crankcase by screws with recessed heads and when these have been removed, the cover can be taken off. This is an operation requiring great care, to avoid unintentional removal of other components. Gently ease off the cover so that the camplate is not disturbed, and at the same time thumb pressure should be applied to the spindle ends to retain them in their normal positions. The timing gears will now be exposed, and they are marked as shown in Fig. 17.

GENERAL MAINTENANCE

When reassembling it must be remembered that the ignition timing should be checked, in case it has moved following slackening of its clip (see page 24) and also that the gearbox must be replenished with oil (see page 9).

250 STAR (AFTER 1964), BARRACUDA AND STARFIRE. Access to the valve-timing gears is obtained in a manner similar to that already described, except for two important differences. Firstly, the contact-breaker assembly must be removed. This involves taking out the two mounting-plate nuts (Fig. 12 or 13 according to model), and the central bolt which secures the spindle to the camshaft. This may require the use of a service tool, B.S.A. part No. 61-3761.

Disconnect the lead to the contact-breaker and withdraw the unit. Release the starter-spring anchor bolt, followed by the retaining screws round the perimeter of the cover which can then be taken off, carrying with it the mainshaft, gears, gearchange mechanism, kickstarter quadrant, etc., as a complete unit, an operation which comprises the second important difference compared with the earlier models. Take care of the loose thrust-washer on the end of the layshaft. The valve-timing gears are now exposed, and they are marked as shown in Fig. 17. When re-assembling, it will be necessary for the ignition to be completely re-set as described on page 21. The camshaft bush is located by a small peg to ensure correct alignment of oil holes—a point to be noted if replacing the bush. Examine the oil seals and replace them if in any way faulty.

Air Cleaner. Under normal conditions cleaning should not be necessary under about 2,000 miles. The filtering element should be washed in petrol and thoroughly dried before refitting into the air-cleaner body.

C10L, C11G AND C12 ENGINES. On the early C10L and C11G engines, the filter was of the "pancake" type, and contained a felt element in zig-zag form, around its periphery. The cleaner dismantles into its component parts following removal of the centre screw.

The later type, also used on the C12 engines, is dismantled by prising out the circlip at the rim of the cleaner, the element itself taking the form of a corrugated disc, comprising alternate layers of wire gauze and special fabric. This element was the subject of a modification early in 1956, being replaced by another under Part No. 42-4591.

250 STAR ENGINES. An air cleaner is provided as standard equipment and is concealed within the fairing below the seat. Removal of the cover on the nearside of the machine gives access to the cleaner, which is of similar construction to that just described, and merely requires the circlip Q (see Fig. 19) to be prised out of position for the perforated cover and filter element to be released.

BARRACUDA AND STARFIRE ENGINES. The air filter is of the "pill-box" type and unscrews from the carburettor mouth. The element is accessible following removal of the perforated band which allows the whole unit to be dismantled.

The Chains. It is normal for chains to stretch as the mileage of the machine increases, due to wear and tear, loading, and because of the variable torque delivered by the engine. All this means that there will be a steadily increasing amount of slackness in the chain, and although "play" is essential within reasonable limits, it must not become excessive. The measurement of slackness in a chain is liable to misinterpretation, because even when a chain is absolutely taut, it is possible to strain it up-and-down slightly. Slackness is measured by the total up-and-down play midway between the sprockets, and is the actual free play as felt by the finger tips.

Adjustment of Primary Chain. C10L, C11G AND C12 MODELS. The chain slackness (sometimes called chain tension, although the author feels

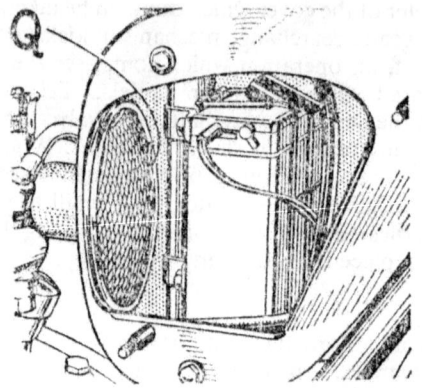

FIG. 19. THE AIR CLEANER ON THE 250 STAR ENGINE

that this is a misleading use of the word "tension") is adjusted by movement of the gearbox, usually rearwards. The gearbox mainshaft projects into the chaincase through a sliding seal, so that adjustment can be made without affecting the chaincase, and it is unnecessary to remove the outer half of the case.

Unscrew the filler cap, when the top run of the chain can be seen, and its slackness gauged with the fingers. If adjustment is required, release the gearbox clamping bolts D (Fig. 20), in the case of the three-speed box, and A (Fig. 21) if a four-speed unit. Move the gearbox backwards and lightly tighten the clamp bolts. Now rotate the engine slowly by operating the kickstarter (and with the sparking plug removed), pausing at intervals to check the chain slackness, which should be $\frac{1}{2}$ in. at the tightest part of the chain. This particular part is specified because primary chains tend to wear irregularly, and if adjusted at a loose position, the tightest part will, in all probability, be too tight.

If the adjustment is satisfactory, screw up the clamp bolts firmly but if not, repeat the above procedure until the desired result is obtained. The

GENERAL MAINTENANCE

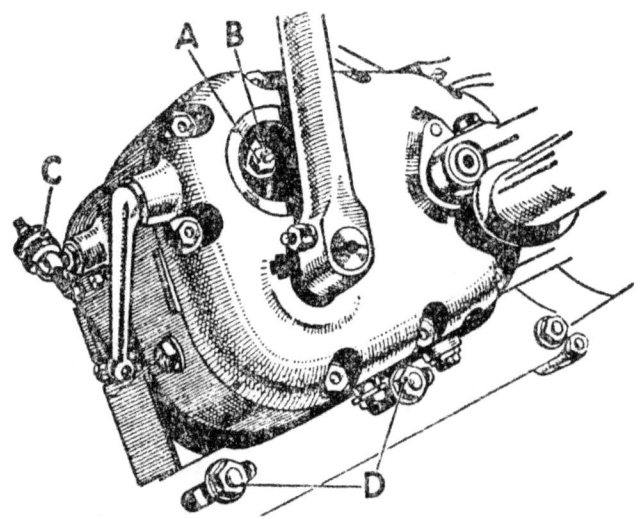

Fig. 20. Clutch and Primary Chain Adjustment on Three-speed Gearbox Models

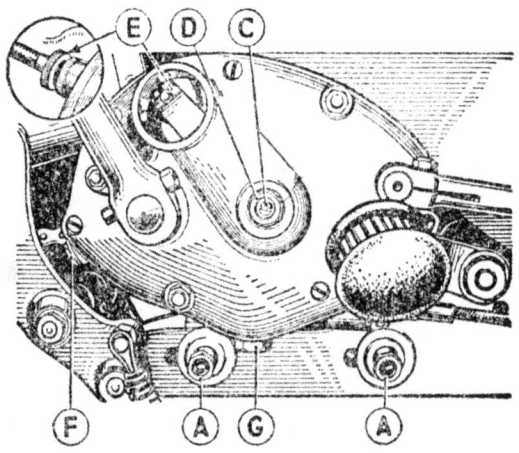

Fig. 21. Clutch and Primary Chain Adjustment on Models with the Light Four-speed Gearbox

clamp bolts must be securely tightened, otherwise the pull in the primary chain may cause the gearbox to slide forward, thus slackening the front chain, and overtightening the rear one. Having adjusted the gearbox position, it will be necessary to re-adjust the rear chain (*see* below).

250 STAR MODEL. The engine and gearbox are built in unit construction and because of the short distance between the sprockets, there is no provision for any adjustment of the chain on earlier models, although an adjuster can be fitted if required. The chain is of the pre-stretched duplex type, and is also "endless," i.e. there is no spring link connexion.

On Scrambles models from engine No. 3001, SS80 engines, and all engines from 1965, (including Barracuda and Starfire engines), a slipper-type adjuster is fitted to the lower run of the chain, and this should be set so that there is no more than $\frac{1}{4}$ in. play in the top run.

In no circumstances whatever must the chain be taut. First take off the footrest, which is fitted to a taper shaft and will require a sharp blow to free it after its fixing nut has been removed. This nut has a left-hand thread, and thus unscrews by turning in a clockwise direction. Then drain the chaincase of oil, either by removal of the drain screw (*see* page 8), or by removing all the screws, when the cover can be taken off. Two of the nuts which retain the alternator stator also lock the adjuster, and after slackening these two nuts, the slipper can be re-set as required. Remember to replace the red screws in their correct position, and to replenish the case with oil (*see* page 8).

Rear Chain Adjustment. Excessive slackness in the rear chain is taken up by sliding the rear wheel spindle rearwards in the slotted fork ends, until the correct slackness is obtained. On machines with rear suspension (of whatever type), the travel of the wheel is not on a true radius centred on the gearbox sprocket, and the chain slackness figures quoted are those to be used when the machine is on its stand, when the wheel will be at its lowest position.

UNSPRUNG FRAME MODELS. First, it will be necessary to slacken the brake adjuster so that the brake rod will not prevent free movement of the wheel, and the bolt anchoring the brake plate to the frame. Next release the wheel-spindle nuts. The speedometer worm-drive unit D, Fig. 22, is locked by nut C, and this must be released, allowing the cable drive to re-align itself when the spindle moves. Turn the wheel until the chain is at its tightest point. It will be noted that one end of the spindle has a square shank, to which a spanner can be applied and turned slowly until the chain slackness has a total up-and-down movement of $\frac{3}{4}$ in. at the centre of the chain. Make sure the cams are firmly against their stops and tighten the speedometer drive locknut, followed by the wheel-spindle nuts—nearside nut first. It is most important that the brake-plate securing bolt is securely locked; if it becomes loose and is lost, the brake cannot be operated. Movement of the wheel invariably upsets the brake adjustment, and this will be a good opportunity to reset the brake as described on page 33.

GENERAL MAINTENANCE 31

PLUNGER SUSPENSION MODELS. Adjustment of the rear wheel position on machines fitted with plunger-type suspension is similar to that for machines without rear suspension insofar as, first the brake adjuster D (Fig. 23)

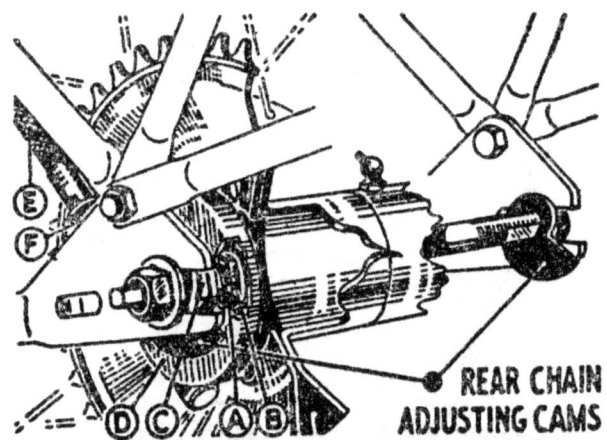

FIG. 22. REAR CHAIN ADJUSTMENT ON UNSPRUNG FRAME MODELS

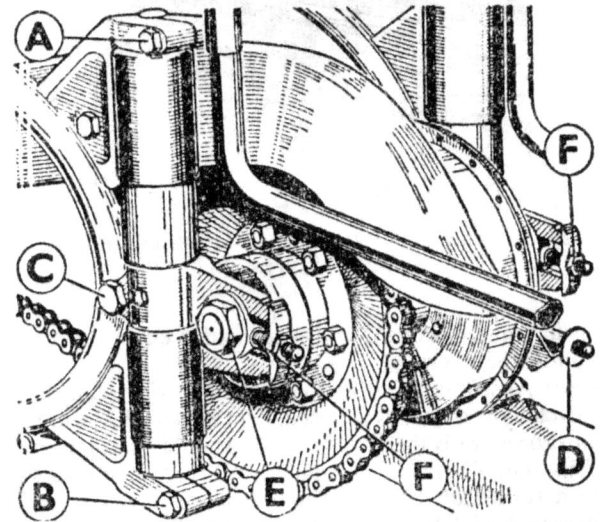

FIG. 23. REAR CHAIN ADJUSTMENT ON MODELS WITH PLUNGER-TYPE SUSPENSION

must be slackened, then the two spindle nuts E, followed by the locknut of the speedometer worm-drive unit (the latter when a three-speed box is fitted). Here the resemblance ceases, because in place of cams, cycle-type adjusters with eye-bolts are used at each of the spindle ends.

Again, rotate the wheel until the tightest point on the chain is found, and tighten the adjuster nuts F, so that the wheel is moved rearwards until the slackness of the chain is ½ in. Take the greatest care to see that movement of the wheel spindle is equal on both sides, to keep the wheel in correct alignment with the frame.

Now re-tighten the spindle nuts and adjust the brake setting as described on page 33. It will also be a good idea to check the wheel alignment (*see*

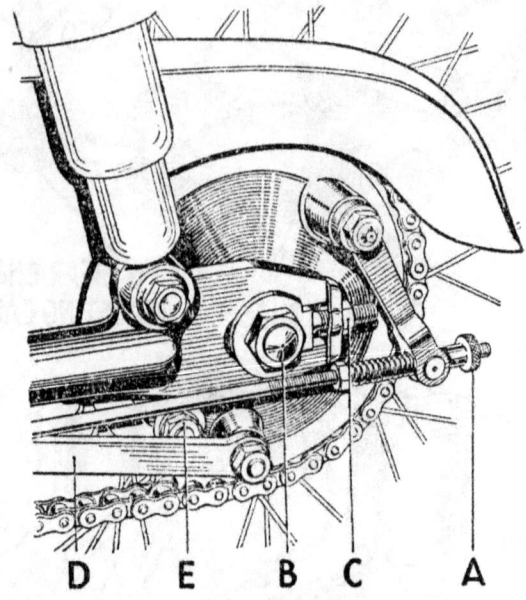

Fig. 24. Rear Chain Adjustment on Models with "Swinging Arm" Suspension

page 33) as any mis-alignment will cause undue chain and tyre wear and adversely affect the steering.

"Swinging Arm" Suspension Models. As with plunger suspension machines, cycle-type adjusters are used, but the main difference in the chain adjustment procedure is that the slackness should be appreciably greater, namely 1⅛ in. On all models, except the 250 Star, the brake shoe plate is fitted with a slotted anchorage which is self-adjusting according to the position of the wheel, but on 250 Star machines, the plate is attached to the "swinging arm" by means of a link D (*see* Fig. 24), and the nuts at both ends require slackening to enable the link to re-align itself in accordance with the new position of the wheel. Tighten the link nuts firmly after the chain adjustment is complete, because if the link becomes disconnected the brake will become useless. Securely tighten the spindle nuts and re-adjust the brakes as detailed below.

GENERAL MAINTENANCE

On Barracuda and Starfire models, although the rear wheel is of the quickly-detachable type, the method and amount of chain adjustment is the same as for the 250 Star. When tightening the spindle nuts, be sure to tighten the near-side one first. Adjust the rear brake as detailed below.

Checking Chain Wear. Lay the chain on a flat surface, such as the top of a bench, and fix one end of the chain. Draw the chain out straight and mark the position of its free extremity. Now compress the chain, and measure the distance between the two positions of the free end of the chain. This is the amount by which the chain has stretched, and should it exceed 2 per cent of the original length the chain should be replaced. The degree of the stretch mentioned is equivalent to a compressed length of 100 pitches being stretched to 102 pitches, or in the case of the primary chain, 50 pitches being stretched to cover 51 pitches. A pitch is the distance between the centres of two adjacent rollers.

It is a waste of money to fit a new chain to worn sprockets, and these should be examined and replaced if necessary. Remember, too, when the chain is refitted, to fasten the spring link with its closed end pointing in the direction of travel of the chain, i.e. forwards on the top run.

Wheel Alignment. It has already been stressed that wheel alignment is of great importance in preventing undue chain wear and in ensuring accurate steering. Time spent on checking the alignment, following rear chain adjustment or wheel removal is well worth while.

A simple gauge is easily made and with its aid checking becomes quick and accurate. A narrow wooden plank is all that is required, with one edge planed straight, and pieces cut out to clear various portions of the machine, such as the central stand. Apply the gauge immediately below the silencer, and keep it in an horizontal position, when the straight edge should touch each tyre at two points.

Brake Adjustment. Ideally, the brake shoes should be set so that they are close enough to the drum for immediate contact when the brake is applied, and yet sufficiently clear not to rub when the pedal is released. The latter is important, of course, because if the shoes rub on the drum, it will become excessively hot, and may even cause the hub grease to melt and possibly run onto the brake linings. The greatest leverage is applied to the shoes when the brake rod (or cable) and the cam lever on the brake plate are at 90 degrees to each other, with the brake "on." If the shoes are worn sufficiently for the angle between the lever and rod to exceed this figure, further life may be obtained from the linings by removing the cam lever, and turning it back by one serration. This does not apply to the front brake of the 250 Star, or to the 1968 Barracuda and Starfire models, where the lever has a square, tapered hole, and should not be disturbed.

The rear brakes on all models have finger adjustment at the lever on the brake cover plate (D, Fig. 23, A, Fig. 24). Note that the knurled adjusting nut is specially shaped to fit the pivot pin, giving a self-locking action, so that the brake cannot slacken off under road shocks.

The front brakes are also adjusted at the brake cover plate (or lower fork leg according to model), but in this case, before the adjuster can be unscrewed, the finger locknut must be slackened off from the face of the cable stop. On the 250 Star and 1968 Starfire, the only adjustment for the front brake is at the handlebar lever, whereas the 1967 Barracuda and Starfire models have brake cables with adjusters at *both* ends.

STARFIRE (1969–70). The front brake is of the two leading-shoe type, operated in the normal manner by cable. In addition to the standard adjuster at the handlebar lever (which, it should be emphasized, is for fine adjustment only), the main adjuster is midway in the cable as shown at B in Fig. 27A.

When the brake shoes have been renewed or re-lined, it will be necessary to "balance" the shoes, otherwise one will carry an excessive load and, in all probability, give inferior braking.

First, disconnect the link-rod C by removal of one pivot pin, and slacken the locknut at the clevis, so that the rod length can be adjusted as required. Apply the brake firmly with the aid of a very strong elastic band wrapped round the handlebar lever and the twist-grip. This is in order to keep the brake applied and at the same time leave the hands free for other work.

Turn the rearmost brake lever (on the cover plate) with a spanner in its normal direction of rotation, until the brake shoe is firmly in contact with the drum. (It is, of course, independent of the front shoe, which is already firmly applied.) Adjust the length of the link rod so that the pivot pin will just pass through the clevis and brake lever.

Secure the pin with either a locknut or split-pin according to model, but whichever method is used, do not omit the securing device—your life may depend on it. Carefully adjust the brake at the adjuster in the cable, bearing in mind the remarks at the beginning of the paragraph.

Replacing the Brake Shoes. The time arrives, inevitably, when the brake linings will have become excessively worn, and it will no longer be possible to adjust the brakes.

The wheel must obviously be removed from the machine (*see* page 35), and the brake shoe plate laid on a bench. Take off the cam lever A (Fig. 25), and press spindle B inwards slightly, allowing the shoes to become clear of the brake plate. The cam levers can be replaced on a new serration if required, except the front lever on the 250 Star and on the 1968 Starfire model.

Now part the shoes a little by inserting a screwdriver between them at the fulcrum pin C, and giving it a twist. A lever, D, can then be applied between one shoe and the cover plate, and the shoe prised off the plate until the spring tension is released, thus freeing both shoes.

Re-lining the shoes is a job within the scope of the amateur mechanic, but one which is just not worth the time and trouble involved. Most lining manufacturers operate a re-lining service at a modest charge.

Replacement of the new shoes need not be difficult. First lay the shoes

GENERAL MAINTENANCE

on the bench and connect the springs. Place the ends of the shoes in their correct positions on the fulcrum pin and cam lever, but with the shoes forming a "vee" between them, about 2 in. away from the brake plate. Then, with the palm of each hand on a shoe, press downwards and outwards until the springs pull the shoes into position.

As an added refinement, the fulcrum pin on the C11G (1955), C12 and 250 Star models is adjustable, so that when the cover plate and shoes have been re-fitted into the drum, slacken the fulcrum-pin nut E (Fig. 24), and operate the cam lever in the normal way to expand the shoes in the drum. The pin will then move until the shoe pressure is equalized. Re-tighten the fulcrum-pin nut in its new position before releasing the lever.

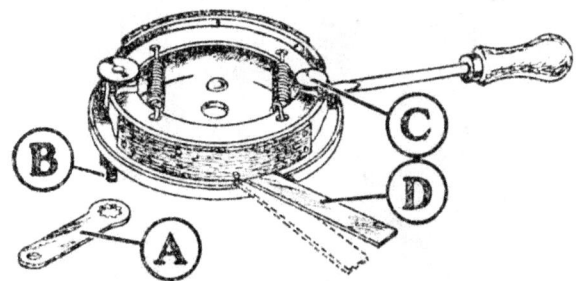

FIG. 25. REMOVING THE BRAKE SHOES

Front Wheel Removal and Replacement. C10L (1954–5) MODELS. First, disconnect the brake cable at its lever on the brake plate. It is quickly detachable and if the cam lever is operated by hand, the cable will become sufficiently slack for it to be withdrawn through the slot in the toggle-end. Unscrew the cable adjuster from the brake plate, when the cable will be disconnected from the wheel. Now take off the two spindle nuts. The brake anchor plate, which is part of the cover plate, is slotted, and the slot is of such a size that the anchor plate cannot pass the fork leg-end and allow the wheel to be taken out at this stage. The next step is to remove all the mudguard stay bolts at the fork leg-end on the opposite side (i.e. the nearside of the machine). Raise the nearside fork leg, which means, in effect, compressing the fork spring, and this will provide sufficient clearance for the wheel to be withdrawn at an angle from the offside fork leg. Replacing the wheel does not call for any special comment and is a matter of straightforward reassembly.

C10L (1956–7) AND C11G (1954) MODELS. First disconnect the brake cable at its lever on the brake plate as described in the previous paragraph, but there is no need to unscrew the cable adjuster, as this is on the fork leg and will not affect removal of the wheel.

The wheel spindle D (Fig. 26) is locked by the pinch bolt A, which is fitted to the nearside fork leg only, and must be slackened. It is now simply a matter of unscrewing the spindle and at the same time supporting the wheel by hand, in order to take its weight off the spindle. The latter passes through the split bush C, which registers in the fork end, and with the removal of the spindle, the bush should be pushed outwards to provide clearance for wheel removal.

It is important to note that the spindle has a left-hand thread, and therefore unscrews by turning in a clockwise direction. When replacing the wheel, make certain that the brake shoe plate stud is located correctly in its socket on the fork leg, otherwise the brake will be inoperative.

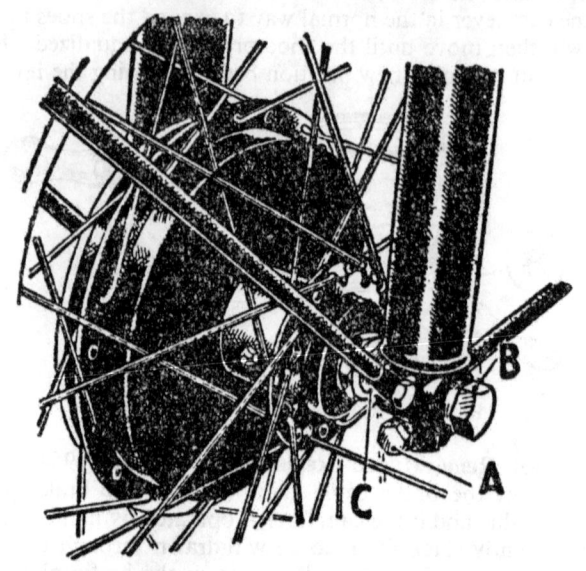

Fig. 26. Front Wheel Removal on 1954 C11G, 1956-7 C10L, and 1967 Barracuda and Starfire Models

Replacing the wheel also calls for special attention to prevent faulty fork action. When the spindle has been replaced and tightened up, do not re-tighten the pinch bolt immediately. Re-connect the brake cable, apply the brake, and depress the forks two or three times to enable the nearside fork leg to align itself on the spindle. When the fork action is satisfactory, tighten the pinch bolt as a final operation.

C11G (1955), C12, Barracuda and Starfire Models (1967). The method of removing the front wheel is the same as that for the 1954 C11G models except that the hexagon spindle-head, B, is replaced by a tommy-bar hole, and the split bush C is non-existent.

Once the wheel is out of the forks, it will be noticed that a sleeve projects from the centre of the brake-drum side of the hub and although it is a tight fit in the hub, if it accidentally receives a sharp blow it may be pushed into the interior of the hub. In this event, the sleeve can be retrieved and repositioned with the aid of the wheel spindle.

GENERAL MAINTENANCE

250 STAR MODELS. Slacken off the front brake cable-adjuster at the handlebar lever and disconnect the cable at the lever on the brake plate, which requires removal of the split pin A (*see* Fig. 27) and pivot pin B or alternatively, a set-screw and nut. Withdraw the cable from its abutment C, in which it is a push-fit. The wheel spindle is retained by caps D on the fork legs and as the cap bolts are unscrewed, the wheel should be supported by hand, to avoid damage to the threads.

The brake plate is prevented from rotating when the brake is applied, by registration of the tongue E on the inside of the fork leg with a slot formed on the plate, and it is most important to see that when the wheel is replaced, the tongue is properly located. Another important point is that of the wheel position, which must be such that the spindle nut F is firmly against the fork end, leaving clearance at the opposite side of the hub. Tighten the cap bolts securely, and when replacing the brake cable, examine the split-pin and replace if found to be faulty.

BARRACUDA AND STARFIRE MODELS (1968). Similar instructions to those for the 250 Star apply to these models except that the spindle is grooved to locate the fork end-cap bolts. A larger brake is specified on these machines.

STARFIRE MODELS (1969-70). An entirely new brake of 7 in. diameter, Fig. 27A, incorporating two leading-shoes was introduced for these years, but the same method of removal is used as for the previous Starfire models.

The clevis at the end of the operating cable on the 1969 brake is secured to the brake plate lever by a combined pivot pin and spring clip. If the latter is damaged in any way during removal, the standard type of pivot pin (with washer and split pin) may be used as a replacement.

As with the earlier Starfire models, the wheel position is determined by grooves in the spindle, in which the end-cap bolts are located.

Wheel Bearing Adjustment. The majority of wheels are fitted with ball journal bearings, for which no adjustment is required, or even possible. The exceptions are the C11G (1954, rear and $5\frac{1}{2}$ in. front, sprung and unsprung frames) and the C10L (1956, front only).

These models have cup-and-cone bearings, the setting of which requires great care to avoid damage to the ball tracks. Whilst adjustment can be made with the wheel in the forks, the most satisfactory way of adjusting the bearings is to take the wheel out of the forks. Fig. 28 shows the adjustable cone B and locknut A. Unlock A and adjust the cone (usually inwards) until there is just perceptible play in the bearings. Make sure the locknut is tight and re-check the setting. The cone must not be overtightened and when the wheel is replaced it should be possible to spin it freely, and the slight play in the bearings should be felt at the rim.

Rear Wheel Removal and Replacement. On all models prior to the introduction of the Barracuda and Starfire models in 1967, the first requirement is to remove the rear chain. Disconnect the spring link, and unwind the chain from the rear sprocket by gently turning the wheel. It will save time and trouble if the chain be left in position on the gearbox

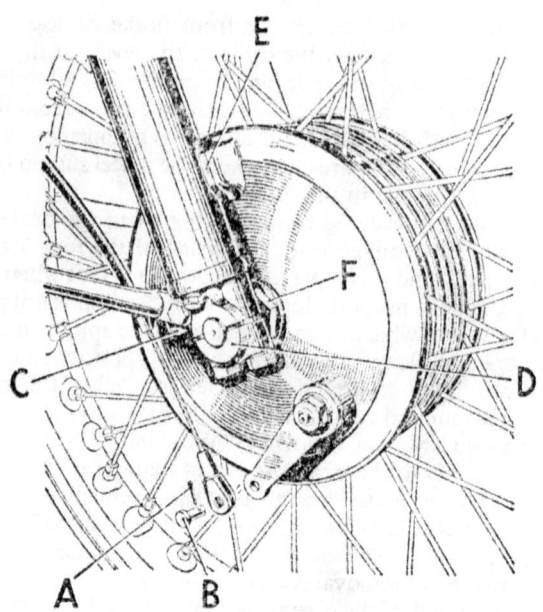

Fig. 27. Front Wheel Removal on the 250 Star Model

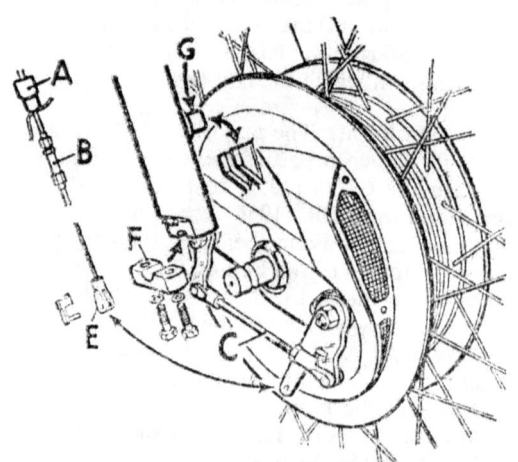

Fig. 27A. Removal of the Front Wheel on the 1969–70 Starfire

sprocket, the loose ends of the chain hanging down and resting on a cloth or other form of protection from grit.

Next, unscrew the brake adjuster from the end of the rod, and if the speedometer is driven from a worm unit at the rear wheel, the cable can be

GENERAL MAINTENANCE

disconnected at the point where it joins the unit, leaving the latter undisturbed on the spindle. When a four-speed gearbox is fitted to the C10L, C11G and C12 machines, a cup replaces the speedometer unit and this, too, can remain untouched. Slacken the wheel-spindle nuts without actually removing them from the spindle, and withdraw the wheel.

Take care not to disturb the setting of the chain adjusters while the wheel is out of the frame and when the wheel is replaced make certain that the

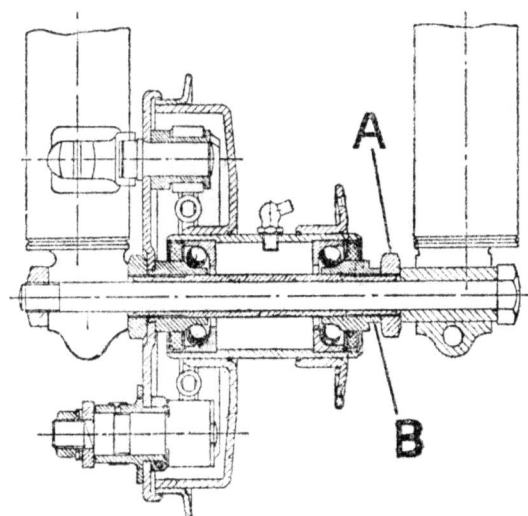

FIG. 28. ADJUSTMENT OF HUBS WITH CUP-AND-CONE BEARINGS

adjusters are pressed firmly against the ends of the forks (or the stops, in case of cam-type adjusters). It is difficult to be certain that these have not moved and it will be advisable to check the chain slackness and the wheel alignment, after the wheel has been replaced (*see* pages 30 and 33).

With two exceptions, the brake shoe plate is slotted to accept a stud attached to the frame, so that the wheel can be either adjusted or removed without effecting its anchorage, and the slotted plate must be properly located on the stud when the wheel is replaced in the frame.

The exceptions are on the 250 Star (*see* below), and on the unsprung frames, where the brake plate is bolted to the frame. Make certain that this bolt is not forgotten after reassembly is completed.

C11G MODELS. These are the only machines on which the tail portion of the rear mudguard is hinged to facilitate wheel removal. The rear stays have slotted ends, and once the nuts are released, the tail unit, complete with rear lamp and number plate, can be lifted upwards.

250 STAR MODELS. Whereas all the other models have the rear brake plate anchored to the frame by a stud or bolt, here a link is used (D, Fig. 24), and this must be detached before the wheel can be moved.

BARRACUDA AND STARFIRE MODELS. These are fitted with quickly-detachable rear wheels and hence neither brake nor chain adjustment is effected when the wheel is removed. Disconnect the speedometer drive at the hub and unscrew the spindle D (Fig. 29). Remove the sleeve E and pull the wheel away from the brake drum, when it will be free for removal.

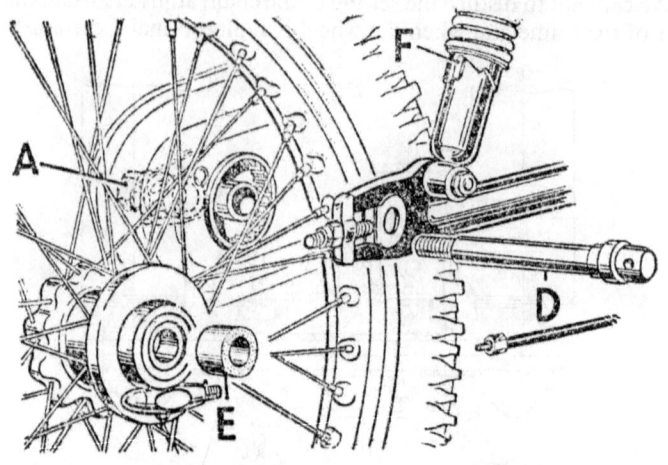

FIG. 29. REMOVING THE REAR WHEEL ON BARRACUDA AND STARFIRE MODELS

The nut A on the near side of the wheel spindle must not be released because it retains the drum in position. Take great care that the chain adjuster nuts are not moved and that the adjusters themselves are correctly located on the fork ends when the wheel is replaced.

3 The Clutch and Gearbox

THE clutch is housed within the chainwheel mounted on the gearbox mainshaft and is totally enclosed in the primary chaincase. It consists of several annular discs, half of which are plain and are assembled alternately with the other half, which carry pads of friction material. The latter plates are keyed to the chainwheel and, therefore, to the engine (via the primary chain), by means of tongues on the periphery of the plates. The plain plates are keyed by similar tongues to the hub of the clutch, which in turn is keyed to the gearbox mainshaft. When the clutch is engaged all the plates are compressed together under the combined pressure of either three or four springs according to model, and rotate as a unit. To disengage the clutch, the plates are separated by means of a push-rod acting on the outer plate which is pressed outwards against the spring pressure.

Both types of gearbox, whether three-speed or four-speed, operate on the same principle. The "drive" enters the box via the clutch and the mainshaft which are keyed together. Parallel with the mainshaft is the shorter layshaft, and both of these carry three (or four) pairs of pinions, having varying numbers of teeth and in constant engagement with each other (hence the term constant mesh gearbox). One of these pinions is extended through a sleeve to the rear chain sprocket outside the gearbox; any pair of pinions can be selected by means of sliding forks operated from the gearchange pedal, enabling different gear ratios to be obtained. Reference to Fig. 30 should make this clear. The pairs of gears are chosen by moving one of the sliding pinions along its shaft until special teeth, formed on the end face and known as "dogs," register with holes in the mating gear, thus causing them to rotate together. The sliding gear rotates with the shaft on "splines" (a series of parallel keys), and is moved laterally by the selector fork. First and top gears are shown, and in the former case the layshaft sliding pinion engages a mating pinion, whilst the mainshaft sliding pinion is disengaged. For top gear, the layshaft sliding gear is disengaged and the mainshaft sliding gear is engaged directly with the sleeved pinion connected to the final-drive sprocket.

Adjustment of Clutch Operation. It is usually obvious when the clutch requires attention, by such symptoms as noisy gear changing, difficulty in engaging gear quietly when at a standstill and a tendency for the machine to move forwards with the clutch disengaged. This means that the clutch is not disengaging properly and is "dragging," a condition usually caused by wear, or incorrect setting of the operating mechanism. Alternatively, wear of the clutch plates may take up all the required clearance in the control mechanism and so cause clutch slip.

Previously, it has been indicated that the clutch is controlled by a push-rod, acting on the clutch pressure plate, and the other end of the rod is operated by a ball thrust pad, set in a cable-operated actuating arm. It is essential that there is a small amount of clearance between the thrust ball and the rod end, otherwise there will be constant pressure on the clutch,

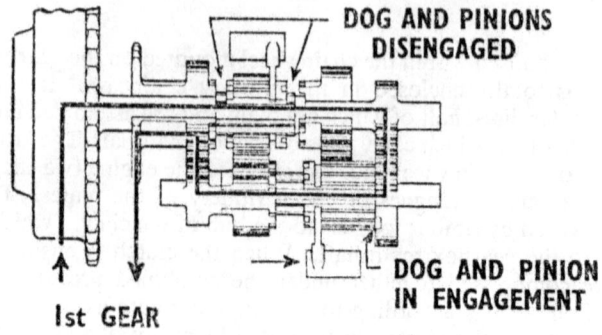

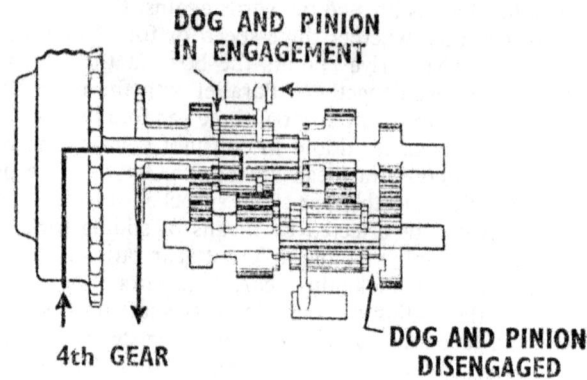

FIG. 30. GEAR WHEEL DISPOSITION ON FIRST AND FOURTH GEARS IN A TYPICAL GEARBOX

causing slip and wear. This same clearance means that there will be a small amount of free play (say 1/16 in.), at the clutch lever on the handlebar.

THREE-SPEED GEARBOX (1954–5 C10L AND C11G) AND FOUR-SPEED GEARBOX (1954–5 C11G). Access to the thrust ball and adjusting screw is obtained via the inspection cover which is screwed in position on the three-speed box, and on the four-speed box takes the form of a plate retained by two screws. The main operating lever is outside the gearbox, and its shaft carries a much shorter lever inside. This in turn carries the thrust ball adjusting screw B (Fig. 20). Slacken the lock nut A sufficiently to allow movement of the screw, and adjust with a screwdriver until there is

THE CLUTCH AND GEARBOX

just a trace of play between the push-rod end and the ball. Check this clearance after the locknut has been tightened. Provision is made at C for adjustment to the cable length, at the lower end of the cable at the gearbox.

LIGHT FOUR-SPEED GEARBOX (1956–8 C10L, C12). The operating lever is enclosed within the gearbox cover. Remove the inspection cap to expose the slotted end of the lever, where there should be approximately $\frac{3}{16}$ in. between the back of the lever and the inside of the cover when the handlebar lever is released, i.e. when the clutch is fully engaged. Any appreciable variation from this figure means that the central pin C (Fig. 21), must be re-set until the correct clearance is obtained. The pin is actually the pivot on which the lever hinges and, therefore, screwing inwards reduces the clearance. Finally, adjust the cable slackness by the finger control behind the cover, until there is about $\frac{1}{16}$ in. of free play at the handlebar end of the lever.

250 STAR GEARBOX. The clutch operating arm is enclosed within the outer timing cover on the offside of the engine. No adjustment is provided at the lever, and the adjustable thrust screw is situated in the centre of the clutch pressure plate on the nearside of the engine.

Remove the chaincase inspection cover, slacken the locknut and adjust the pin with a screwdriver until all free motion is just taken up. This must be done without the use of force, to avoid the risk of separating the clutch plates. Before tightening the locknut, slacken the screw back half a turn to restore the normal working clearance. This will automatically give a little free play at the handlebar lever, where still finer adjustment of the cable length is provided. Note that the operating lever on the offside must not contact the inside of the cover when the clutch is engaged, and if there is any doubt about this, the cover must be removed and the lever repositioned by alteration of both handlebar and thrust screw adjustment.

250 STAR (AFTER 1964), BARRACUDA AND STARFIRE GEARBOXES. On these models the clutch control is by a "rack and pinion" mechanism. The control is in correct adjustment when, with the handlebar lever released, the short lever above the timing case is inclined outwards by a small amount. The lever should be approximately parallel with the cover-joint face when the handlebar lever is gripped. To obtain this condition adjust the thrust screw at the centre of the clutch pressure plate as described above.

Access to the Clutch. This is a straightforward dismantling operation, after first draining the oil from the case (page 8). Remove the footrests, and on the C10L, C11G and C12 models, take out all the screws round the rim of the case together with the two screws which secure it to the gearbox shield (where fitted). The nuts for these screws are welded on and so cannot be lost. Take careful note of the positions of the washers and distance pieces for replacement purposes.

On 250 Star, Barracudas, and Starfires up to 1969, the footrest is retained by a nut having a left-hand thread and must be turned clockwise to unscrew it. (This does not apply to 1970 Starfire models.) The screws at the rim of the cover require a special screwdriver before they can be released and the use of this tool will be even more important when tightening them afterwards. It now remains to depress the brake pedal and take off the cover.

On all models, do not forget to replenish the chaincase with oil (page 8).

Clutch Spring Pressure (C10L, C11G, C12 MODELS). Spring loading is pre-determined so that adjustment is unnecessary, and the three screws should be screwed up tightly.

250 STAR, BARRACUDA AND STARFIRE MODELS. The four spring sleeve-nuts P (Fig. 32) are individually adjustable and normally each nut should be positioned so that the underside of the head is about $\frac{1}{16}$ in. from the face of the spring cup, when the plates are new. This figure is given as a guide only and it is a simple matter to vary it according to circumstances. It should be borne in mind that if the springs are compressed excessively, the handlebar lever will be stiff to operate and, alternatively, if the spring pressure is not sufficient, the clutch will tend to slip.

At the same time that this adjustment is made, check that the plates run parallel with each other when the clutch is disengaged, because if not, this can be one of the causes of clutch "drag" and noisy gear engagement. Depress the clutch handlebar lever and operate the kickstarter, so that the plates rotate without turning the engine, when it can be seen whether the plates spin truly. If the plates wobble, the spring nuts must be adjusted separately, until each spring exerts the same pressure and true running is obtained.

Renewing the Clutch Plates. Only partial dismantling of the clutch is necessary for examination of the plates, and both clutch hub and chainwheel can remain in position on the gearbox mainshaft. Unscrew the spring nuts, thus releasing the spring pressure, and remove the outer (or pressure) plate L (Fig. 32), which carries the springs and their cups. The plates should be extracted singly and drawn out as squarely as possible to avoid jamming on either the chainwheel or the hub. If any difficulty is experienced in removing the plates, a tool resembling the old-fashioned button hook should be made from a piece of wire.

Examine the plates and if the steel ones are scored they must be replaced by new ones. Note that in the C10L, C11G and C12 clutches, one steel plate is thicker than the others, and this is the first to be inserted when reassembling. The plates are of equal thickness on the C15 clutches, but a steel plate is still the first to be inserted. As a guide to the amount of wear which has taken place on the friction plates of the C10L, C11G and C12 clutches, the cork inserts were $\frac{3}{16}$ in. thick (overall) when new. Friction plates on the 250 Star, Barracuda and Starfire, are fitted with their pads bonded in position, and the extent to which they have worn can be gauged by the fact that they were $\frac{1}{32}$ in. thick when new. If the pads are excessively worn, or glazed, or show signs of burning, they should be replaced.

THE CLUTCH AND GEARBOX

In the case of the cork inserts, new corks can be obtained, but will require machining to give a perfectly flat disc.

As the new friction plates will be thicker than the ones which have been taken out, the clutch operation will require re-setting in accordance with the details given on page 41.

Clutch Shock Absorber. Situated in the hub of the clutch, the shock absorber is a device which allows an initial limited amount of rotary slip between the driving and driven members of the clutch. It consists of synthetic rubber blocks sandwiched between vanes, the rubber compressing under sudden loading.

When the time comes for replacement of the rubber blocks, the clutch must be dismantled completely (*see* page 46) and the old rubbers removed.

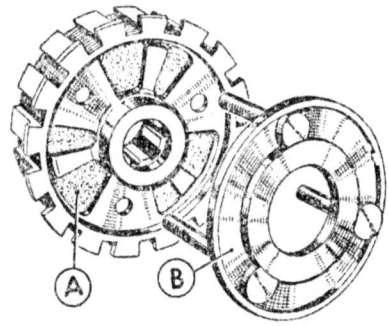

FIG. 31. ASSEMBLY OF THE CLUTCH SHOCK ABSORBER RUBBERS
On later models the rubber blocks are of equal thickness

Fitting new rubbers is not too difficult a task, but a little ingenuity may be required in the absence of special tools for the job. The vaned centre should be held as if mounted on a vertical shaft and if a strip of steel $\frac{3}{4}$ in. wide by $\frac{3}{16}$ in. thick is clamped upright in a vice, the centre can be held on this. (The size of strip for the 250 Star clutch centre should be $1\frac{3}{16}$ in. by $\frac{1}{2}$ in.) Next, place the hub in position together with the thick rubbers A, correctly located as shown in Fig. 31. Turn the hub so as to compress the rubbers slightly and slip the thinner rubbers into position. The hub can be turned if an old clutch plate is converted into a "spanner," by the addition of a lever about 12 in. long. Replace the back cover plate B, together with the bolts, and in the case of the 250 Star Model clutch add the front cover plate which is held by four screws.

A mid-season modification to the 250 Star clutch shock absorber was introduced at engine No. 41778, and at engine No. 3028 for the Sport Star, SS80. Eight rubber blocks of equal thickness superseded those of two different thicknesses and the vaned components were modified to suit. The new shock absorber unit remains interchangeable with the previous type and its use is continued on the Barracuda and Starfire Models.

Removal and Replacement of the Clutch. The first stage in dismantling the clutch is described in the section dealing with the renewal of the clutch plates.

C10L, C11G AND C12 MODELS. After the plates have been removed, the next step is to disconnect the primary chain. Rotate the engine by means of the kickstarter until the spring link is on the top run of the chain and opposite a recess in the back half of the case. Remove the "hairpin" spring, when the link can be pushed through into the recess, specially provided for this purpose and for reinsertion of the link when reassembly takes place.

The clutch is retained on the mainshaft by two nuts, one behind and the other with a washer in between. The outer nut has a left-hand thread and thus unscrews by turning in a clockwise direction. The clutch centre is mounted on a splined portion of the gearbox mainshaft, and can be withdrawn without the aid of an extractor. The chainwheel runs on uncaged roller bearings and the removal should be carried out with great care to make sure that the bearings do not fall out. As soon as the chainwheel has been moved sufficiently to enable two fingers to be inserted behind it, the large thrust washer at the back of the clutch can be removed simultaneously, keeping the rollers in position. The split circlip, which was retained by the thrust washer, is also released.

Now part the chainwheel and the clutch hub, taking care not to lose the roller bearings of which there are 18.

It may be as well to dismantle the hub completely, in order to examine the shock-absorber rubbers, and if the three bolts and the back plate are removed, the rubbers and the vaned centre will be exposed. If the rubbers are in poor condition, the vanes and hub will separate easily, but otherwise the centre must be pushed out with the aid of a suitable drift.

Reassembly of the clutch is a straightforward matter. Fit the halves of the split circlip in position (a dab of grease will help here), and replace the thrust washer in position over them. Lay the clutch hub face downwards and position the rollers carefully round their track on the vane centre (again using a little grease to retain them in position), and slide the chainwheel into place over the rollers. Carefully fit the assembly on to the mainshaft and replace the first nut and washer. The nut must be firmly tightened to prevent any endwise movement of the clutch. Now add the outer washer and nut, remembering that this has a left-hand thread.

Replace the plates, the thick plain one being the first to be inserted, and refit the spring assemblies, tightening their nuts down firmly onto the distance pieces. Connect the primary chain, making use of the recess in the back of the case for the insertion of the spring link, and then check the operation of the clutch (*see* page 41). When the chaincase has been reassembled replenish with oil to the correct level.

250 STAR MODELS. Owing to the fact that the gearbox and clutch are built in unit construction with the engine, rather more work is involved in dismantling the clutch. Having reached the stage of removing the primary chaincase cover, the next task is to detach the engine sprocket, chain and

THE CLUTCH AND GEARBOX

chainwheel, as a unit, because the chain is of the "endless" type, and is not fitted with a spring link. This involves taking off the alternator, and its leads must first be disconnected outside the case at the snap connectors, which simply pull apart. Make a note of the cable colours, and draw the lead through the grommet in the back of the case.

The stator, i.e. the stationary portion of the alternator which carries the coils, is retained by three nuts and washers E (Fig. 32), and with these out of the way, the stator can be taken off. A point to note here is that as the fixing holes in the stator are symmetrically disposed, it can be replaced the

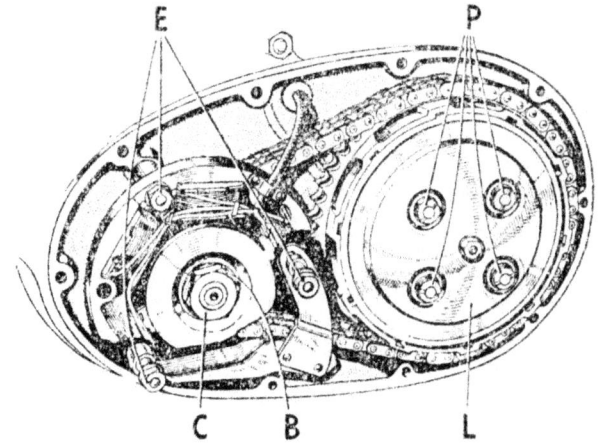

FIG. 32. THE ALTERNATOR AND PRIMARY DRIVE ASSEMBLY ON THE 250 STAR (SIMILAR FOR THE BARRACUDA AND STARFIRE MODELS)

wrong way round. The correct method of assembly is with the lead on the outside of the stator. Competition Models from engines No. C15S-3001, all Sports Stars, all 250 Stars made after 1964, Barracuda and Starfire models, are fitted with a chain tensioner pivoting off the stator studs, so that once the stator itself is removed, the tensioner can be taken out. Make a careful note of the disposition of the distance-pieces.

The rotor, i.e. the inner rotating portion of the alternator, is keyed to the engine mainshaft and locked endwise by nut C, which in turn is prevented from becoming loose by the locking washer B. Straighten the tab of this washer and unscrew the nut which has the normal right-hand thread. It may be difficult to prevent the engine from rotating while releasing this nut and in this event, engage top gear and apply the rear brake while the nut is being unscrewed. Draw the rotor off the shaft and take out the key to avoid its being lost.

The next step is to dismantle the clutch plates as detailed under "Renewing the Clutch Plates," page 44, which will leave the chainwheel and hub still in position. The centre sleeve on which the clutch is mounted is held on the mainshaft by a taper and locked to it by the central nut. This, in turn, is locked by a washer having a tab bent over one of the flats of the nut. Straighten the tab and unscrew the nut. As before, if there is any difficulty in releasing the nut engage top gear and apply the rear brake, while the nut is being unscrewed. Note that the washer has another tongue engaging with the hub and it must be reassembled in the same way. Similarly, the thick washer exposed when the mainshaft nut is removed is recessed on one face, and must be fitted with this face outwards. Next, withdraw the clutch push-rod from the centre of the mainshaft.

It now remains to free the clutch centre from the taper on the mainshaft and provision has been made for this by the addition of a thread to take an

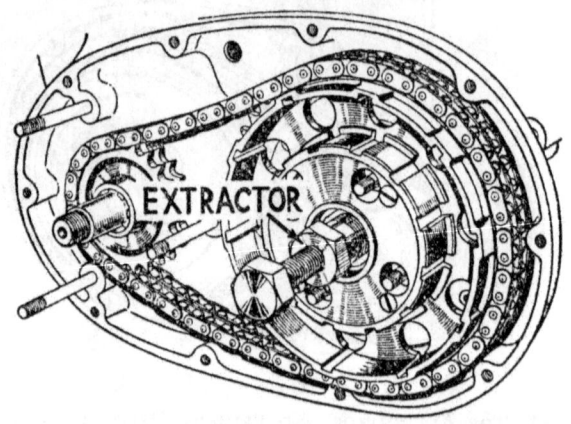

FIG. 33. USING AN EXTRACTOR TO WITHDRAW THE CLUTCH FROM THE GEARBOX MAINSHAFT (250 STAR, BARRACUDA AND STARFIRE MODELS)

extractor (see Fig. 33). The body of the extractor should be screwed into the centre sleeve as far as possible and the bolt then screwed in until it touches the end of the mainshaft. A sharp blow on the spanner applied to the bolt will free the clutch from the shaft. The extractor is B.S.A. Part No. 61-3583 and using it as a handle, the clutch, primary chain, and engine sprocket can be drawn off together, and laid on the bench with the extractor uppermost. Unscrew the extractor, and lift out the clutch hub containing the rubber shock absorbers. This can be dismantled, fitted with new rubbers if required, and reassembled as detailed in the section "Clutch Shock Absorber," page 45.

Reassembly of the clutch and the alternator does not present much difficulty, but there are one or two items worthy of special mention. When the clutch centre and the rotor were drawn off their shafts, driving keys were exposed, and it is important that these are not omitted, otherwise, in the case of the clutch, the drive will be transmitted solely by the interference fit of the centre sleeve on the mainshaft taper, and as a consequence the shaft may be seriously damaged.

THE CLUTCH AND GEARBOX

Further, when the rotor is replaced on its shaft, the recessed face must be to the outside. Note that there is no recess on the Barracuda and Starfire models and the rotor must be replaced with the "Strobelite" timing mark on the *outer* face. The stator leads must also be at the outside at the top. The air gap between the rotor and each of the stator poles should be equal and on no account must these parts be allowed to make contact.

A most important item is that of the clutch mainshaft nut. Although this must be tightened firmly, over-tightening may cause the clutch to drag, and for this reason, the nut should be tightened with a torque spanner set to 65 lb-ft. Few private owners possess such a tool but, if the homely spring balance is applied to the end of the spanner, and the pull measured by this means, a satisfactory result can be obtained. It is perhaps as well to remember that 65 lb-ft represents a 65 lb pull on a spanner 1 ft long, or 130 lb on a spanner 6 in. long, so that a simple calculation will give the poundage for any length of spanner. For accurate readings, the spanner and the direction of pull of the balance must be at 90 degrees to each other.

In addition, the thick washer beneath the mainshaft nut must be placed in position with the recess outwards, and the special tongue on the tab washer must be fitted into the clutch hub. A plain washer is used on the Barracuda and Starfire Models.

Now replace the push-rod. There are four friction plates in the clutch alternately spaced with plain ones, and one of the latter must be replaced first. The pressure plate will then operate against the outer friction plate. Adjustment of the spring pressure and the clutch operation have already been described in previous sections and reference should be made to these. When the chaincase cover is being replaced, the red screws must be put back in their correct places, and the chaincase replenished with oil to the proper level.

BARRACUDA AND STARFIRE MODELS. With only minor differences due to improvements in design, the procedure for removal and replacement of the clutch is the same as for the 250 Star Models.

THE GEARBOXES

In the following sections details are given of the dismantling and re-assembling of the various gearboxes used on the 250 c.c. models, and notes are included on the replacement of the kickstarter and gearchange springs for those who merely wish to replace either of these items. For the private owner it will usually be much more convenient to carry out any dismantling without removing the gearbox from the frame, because, as a rule, only partial dismantling is required. The possible exception to this is if attention is required to the sleeve pinion bearing, but even here the job can be done satisfactorily with a little care. It is, of course, preferable to have the gearbox on the bench, and the time and trouble taken in removing it, will be amply repaid. If such attention is required it will mean that the inner half of the primary chaincase will have to be taken off involving the prior removal of the alternator and engine sprocket.

Removing the Chaincase (Inner Half). C10L, C11G AND C12 MODELS. Remove the mainshaft nut and lock washer, followed by the stator retaining nuts (*see* 250 Star Models, page 47). The stator can then be drawn off its studs but if this proves to be difficult, insert a screwdriver into the chamfer at the back of the alternator housing and gently prise the stator free. The rotor can be removed from the mainshaft next, together with the dished oil-flinger disc, leaving the sprocket on the mainshaft. If the clutch has been dismantled, the primary chain will be out of the way and the sprocket can be pulled off the mainshaft. If the chain is still in position, operate the kickstarter gently until the spring link coincides with the recess in the back of the case and detach the spring link, so uncoupling the chain. The alternator back plate, together with its retaining bolt and the three distance-pieces, can now be taken off and the inner half of the chaincase drawn away from the crankcase after unscrewing its retaining bolts. On earlier models four studs were employed instead of three and the back plate was retained by two nuts. Careful note should be made of the assembly sequence.

With all the gearboxes it will be assumed that the dismantling of the primary chaincase and clutch has already been carried out as detailed in previous sections, and the stage has been reached where the gearbox has been isolated and the bare mainshaft exposed.

Note that a limited number of machines was produced employing a brass shield behind the stator in conjunction with a plain steel washer on the mainshaft, instead of the dished disc. Removal of the clutch is described in the appropriate section. The 250 Star, Barracuda and Starfire models employ an endless chain, so that the clutch chainwheel, primary chain, and engine sprocket must all be removed together, and this is detailed in the section "Removal and Replacement of the Clutch," page 46.

LIGHT FOUR-SPEED GEARBOX (1956-8, C10L AND C12). *To dismantle*—remove the drain plug from the gearbox and while the oil is draining, set the gears in the neutral position, disconnect the speedometer cable and remove the nuts and screws retaining the outer cover. This is positioned by two dowels and may require a sharp tap with a mallet to free it. As the cover comes away, the clutch operating lever will fall free, as its fulcrum pin is set in the cover and the kickstarter lever will swing forward as it comes free of its stop. It is not necessary to remove either kickstarter or gearchange pedals unless their springs are to be replaced.

If the gearchange centralizing spring requires removal, slacken the clip bolt on the lever, and remove it from its spindle together with the circlip behind it. The gearchange mechanism can then be withdrawn and a new spring slipped into position. At the same time examine the operating claw and check that the ends are not unduly worn.

To replace the kickstarter spring, take off the pedal which becomes free on its shaft when the cotter pin is driven out, and withdraw the quadrant. One end of the spring hooks round the end face of the quadrant and the opposite end terminates in an eye fixed to the outer cover by a set pin, which screws through the cover and has a locknut outside. The quadrant return

THE CLUTCH AND GEARBOX

stop is fixed to the inner cover and need not be disturbed. Remove the clutch push-rod from the centre of the mainshaft and unscrew the nut on the end of the mainshaft, so releasing the kickstarter ratchet assembly. Then, unscrew the clutch cable adjuster and move the cable out of the way. The gearbox inner cover is held in position by one nut (just above the mainshaft) and, with its removal and that of the circlip on the layshaft, the inner cover can be taken off, bringing with it the mainshaft and two of its pinions. The layshaft gear and thrust washer can also be removed. The mainshaft can be tapped out of its bearing, leaving the two pinions in

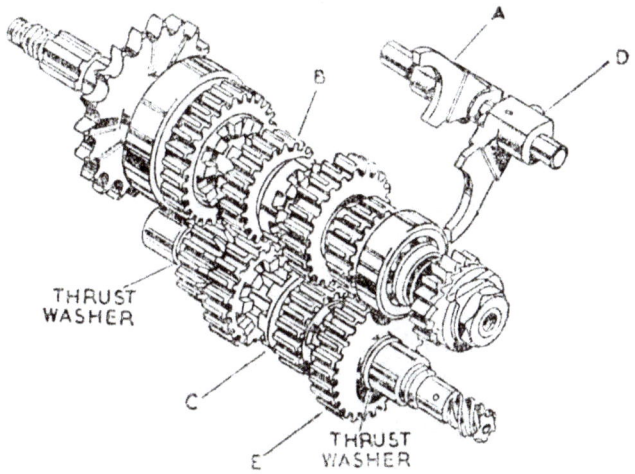

FIG. 34. GEAR CLUSTER IN THE LIGHT FOUR-SPEED GEARBOX

position and these can be pressed off afterwards if required. If either the ball journal bearing or needle-roller bearing needs replacement, warm the cover and push out. Note that the former type of bearing first requires removal of its retaining circlip. The speedometer drive cannot be taken out until its bush is free, and this is held by a securing nut and a retaining pin on the outside of the box. In mid-1958, a sealing ring was added to the bush to prevent oil leaks, and when replacing the bush, care is required to ensure that the sealing ring is not harmed.

The gear control quadrant is also carried by the inner cover and if this is to be removed, first press out the gearchange spindle bush to expose the end of the quadrant spindle. The latter is threaded $\frac{1}{4}$ in. B.S.C., and by using a suitable bolt as an extractor, the spindle can be withdrawn.

The gear selector forks A and D (*see* Fig. 34) are carried on a shaft secured to the gearbox shell by a grub-screw, located on the sleeve pinion boss behind the sprocket. The screw will require a long screwdriver, as it is shielded by the chaincase and other items, and with its removal the shaft can be taken out. This permits the gear cluster forks and layshaft to be withdrawn, so that the only other components remaining are the sleeve pinion and the camplate. The latter can be pulled off its pivot pin, but note that its spring-loaded pawl will be suddenly released unless held back.

To remove the sleeve pinion, straighten the lockwasher and undo the sprocket retaining nut. Application of the rear brake will prevent the sprocket from turning, as the nut is unscrewed. Disconnect the rear chain, remove the sprocket, and drive the sleeve pinion through its bearing and into the gearbox, by means of a mallet. Take care not to damage the oil seal during this operation. On the other hand, if it has shown signs of leakage, prise out its retaining circlip and replace the seal with a new one. If the mainshaft bearing is to be replaced, then the circlip and seal must be removed and the bearing tapped out from inside the box, with the aid of a suitable punch. The shell should be warmed before carrying out this operation, by wrapping in rags which have been immersed in hot water and wrung out.

Wash all parts thoroughly in paraffin and examine for wear. Note especially that the hardened thrust washer at each end of the layshaft (*see* Fig. 34), must be in good condition to prevent excessive end play. Different thicknesses are available if required. Having decided on the parts to be replaced, the process of rebuilding the gearbox can commence.

Reassembly. Once again, warm the gearbox shell, and press the mainshaft bearing into position. Great care is necessary here to ensure that the bearing is inserted as squarely as possible, to avoid jamming and damaging the housing. Refit the oil seal and its circlip, and insert the sleeve pinion into the bearing from the inside of the box. Drive firmly into position. Slide the sprocket very carefully into position to prevent damage to the seal, and replace the rear chain. Refit the locking washer and tighten the ring nut securely. Be sure to drive the locking washer into one of the slots in the ring. The camplate is next to receive attention. Insert the pawl spring into position and raise the pawl, to allow the camplate to be replaced on its pivot. Set the pawl and plate in the first-gear position. There are five notches on the camplate, three of which are close together. The end of these is the first-gear position.

Replace the layshaft with its two innermost gears in position, and the thrust washer in its correct place.

Mount the mainshaft selector fork A (*see* Fig. 34), on its shaft, fitting the latter loosely in position in the gearbox shell, while the fork is positioned with its operating peg in the groove in the camplate. Put the mainshaft sliding pinion B into position on the fork, and add the sliding pinion C on the layshaft. Carefully withdraw the selector fork shaft. Fit the layshaft selector fork D and engage its operating peg in the groove on the camplate. Again replace the fork shaft through the two forks, but this time tighten its locating grub-screw, making sure that it fits properly into the shaft groove.

Slide the mainshaft (complete with its two outer pinions) into position, turning it gently to enable the splines on the shaft to line up with those in the sliding pinion. Now add the layshaft pinion E and its thrust washer.

THE CLUTCH AND GEARBOX

Note that as the camplate is set in first gear, the dogs on the face of the sliding layshaft pinion will engage in holes on the face of pinion E. Now replace the clutch push-rod.

The inner cover is now ready for replacement, but before it is pushed home and the securing nut fitted, a new paper joint should be added, and the selector quadrant must be set in the first-gear position, i.e. the red spot on the cover must register with the red spot on the quadrant (*see* Fig. 35). This is extremely important, otherwise the gear engagement will

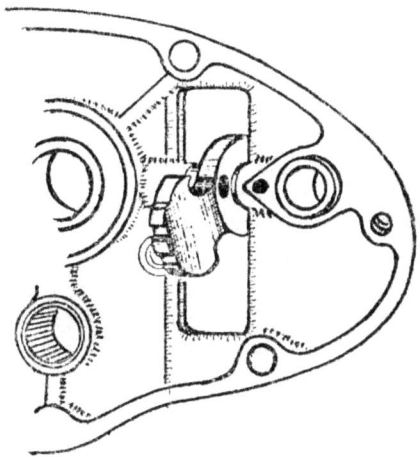

FIG. 35. SETTING THE GEAR-CHANGE QUADRANT

not function properly. As the cover is fitted, the quadrant will be felt to engage with its mating pinion on the back of the camplate.

Reassemble the kickstarter ratchet mechanism and lock up tightly, as this takes up all the end-play in the mainshaft, and secure with the tab washer.

The outer cover, complete with gearchange mechanism and kickstarter can be replaced next, using a new paper joint, and this will require extra care because the kickstarter quadrant has to engage with its gear on the mainshaft and at the same time the speedometer worm drive must engage with its mating pinion on the layshaft.

It will also be advisable to remove the inspection cover to make sure that the clutch operating lever is correctly positioned. Reconnect the speedometer drive and be certain to replace the drain plug. Refill with a recommended grade of lubricant (*see* page 4).

THREE-SPEED GEARBOX (C10L, C11G (1954–5) MODELS). *To dismantle—* remove the drain plug and disconnect the clutch cable. While the gearbox is draining, slacken the pinch bolt on the gearchange pedal and draw it off its shaft. Drive the cotter pin out of the kickstarter crank, and remove it also.

From beneath the gearbox outer cover, unscrew the housing carrying the pawl plate plunger E (Fig. 36), which can then be removed complete with its spring. Next, undo all the nuts and screws retaining the cover and tap it off with a wooden mallet, at the same time holding the gearchange spindle so that the mechanism it carries inside the box is retained in position. With the cover out of the way, unscrew the plunger and housing O from the inner cover, thus releasing the gearchange mechanism assembly. This comprises three main components, the operating plate D, the pawl carrier plate G with spring and pawls J, and the selector quadrant H, all of

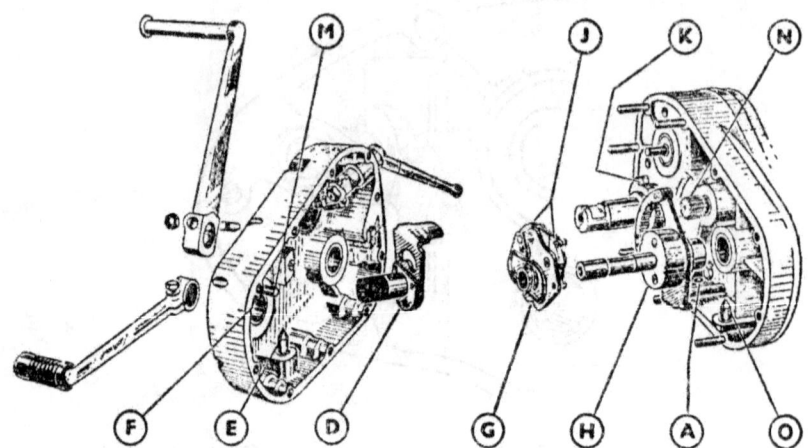

FIG. 36. GEAR-CHANGE MECHANISM IN THE THREE-SPEED GEARBOX

which can be dismantled and the spring replaced if necessary. Note that the right-hand tongue of the pedal-return spring passes to the left of the stud and vice-versa, thus overlapping each other.

The inner cover is held by three bolts and after removing these, the cover can be drawn off the long gearbox studs complete with kickstarter quadrant. The cover is dowelled in position and may require tapping off with a mallet. If it is necessary to fit another kickstarter spring, unscrew its fixing pin in the cover, and drive the quadrant through the two stop plates towards the inner face of the cover, taking care not to damage the cork washer. Any oil leakage at this point should be rectified by a new washer. Check also that the rubber stop is in good condition.

The gear selector fork shaft is grooved at its inner end and is prevented from moving endwise by a retaining pin, and after removing its covering plug on the top of the box, a ¼ in. B.S.F. bolt can be used as an extractor to remove the pin. Draw the clutch push-rod from the centre of the mainshaft. The next step is to withdraw the mainshaft with its sliding gear, the layshaft gear cluster, and the selector shaft with its forks, in one operation.

THE CLUTCH AND GEARBOX

The layshaft will remain in position, as it fits into the back of the gearbox and is locked by an external nut and washer.

The sleeve pinion is still in position, and before this can be removed the sprocket must be taken off. Straighten the locking washer securing the sprocket lock ring, which can then be unscrewed. If there is difficulty in preventing the sprocket from rotating, apply the rear brake, and once the nut is removed the chain can be disconnected. The sprocket can now be drawn off the sleeve pinion and the latter driven from its bearing with the aid of a wooden mallet, into the gearbox shell.

If the ball race is to be renewed, warm the box and tap the bearing from its housing, into the gearbox. This will leave an oil seal exposed, which should be replaced if there is any doubt as to its efficiency. It must be fitted with its recessed face towards the interior of the box.

Turning now to the gear cluster, the mainshaft sliding gear literally slides off the mainshaft and also the kickstarter ratchet assembly when its thin end-nut is unscrewed. This nut has a left-hand thread and therefore is turned clockwise to unscrew it. To remove the remaining pinion on the mainshaft, the retaining ring in its recessed face must be split with the aid of a chisel, so that the ring may be removed in two portions. (The ring is especially notched for this purpose.) The inner ring is already in two pieces and may be extracted with a sharp instrument, such as a knitting needle.

To dismantle the layshaft gear cluster, the large pinion must be removed. It is a press-fit on its pinion sleeve, but can be removed by holding the gear in a vice using soft-faced clams, and tapping out of position with a piece of hard wood slightly larger in diameter than the phosphor-bronze bearing. The selector forks can be removed from their shaft, if the latter is held in a vice and the pegs which operate in the cam grooves are driven out with a suitable punch. The forks are not interchangeable and their respective positions should be noted carefully. The pegs fit into taper holes and as they are also lightly riveted over, will be firmly in position. They must be equally firm when replaced.

Reassembly. As when dismantling, the case must be warmed before the bearing is replaced and remember to insert the oil-seal shim first. Take care to insert the bearing as squarely as possible to avoid jamming and so damaging the housing. Fit the sleeve pinion through the bearing from inside the gearbox and be sure the shim is not omitted from between the bearing and the face of the pinion. Replace the sprocket on the splines of the sleeve pinion, couple the rear chain, and then tighten the lock ring securely. Make certain that the locking washer is turned over into the recesses in the ring.

If the selector forks have been removed, it will be essential to use new pegs for the cam grooves, to enable light riveting to be carried out satisfactorily.

Now replace the small pinion on the mainshaft, fit the two halves of the inner retaining ring, and tap a new ring into position. When this operation is completed the pinion must revolve freely on the shaft. The kickstarter ratchet assembly can be put on the shaft again, and a reminder must be given that the securing nut has a left-hand thread.

Turning next to the shafts, reassemble the sliding pinion on to the mainshaft with the fork groove farthest from the small pinion which has just been replaced. Put the layshaft sliding pinion on to its sleeve pinion, with the fork groove nearest to the pinion and press the large gear on to the hexagon end of the sleeve.

Pair the layshaft and mainshaft gear clusters together, fit the selector forks into their respective grooves, the outer fork engaging with the mainshaft sliding pinion and the inner one with the layshaft sliding pinion.

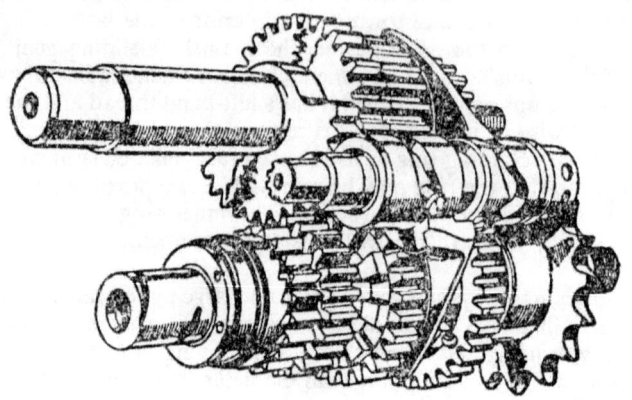

FIG. 37. GEAR CLUSTER IN A THREE-SPEED GEARBOX

Enter the cluster into the box, the mainshaft penetrating the pinion sleeve first, followed by the layshaft gears on to their shaft, and the selector shaft. The latter must be correctly located in the gearbox shell when the retaining pin can be added and secured by its covering plug and locking washer.

With a new joint washer in position, tap the inner cover home and secure it by a bolt on each side. Examine the mainshaft and layshaft for end play. This can be detected in the mainshaft by grasping its exposed end and endeavouring to push it in and out. It should be free to rotate easily but without end play, which can be taken up by the addition of a shim under the head of the mainshaft plain bearing in the cover. Layshaft end play can be detected by endwise movement of the kickstarter spindle. If it exceeds 0·005 in. suitable shims must be fitted between the kickstarter quadrant and the inner face of the cover. When the clearances are correct, tighten all three bolts securely, and then return the clutch push-rod into position.

The gearchange mechanism is next to receive attention. Replace the central quadrant in its bearing and—most important—make sure that the "timing" marks on the selector shaft gear N (*see* Fig. 36), and on the quadrant, coincide. Fit the spring to the pawl carrier plate G, it being essential to fit the right-hand tongue of the pedal-return spring to the left of its anchor stud and vice versa. Refit the carrier plate on to the spindle of the control quadrant H, followed by the operating sleeve D. Reassemble the two return stops K to the kickstarter spindle, add the cork washer (preferably a new one) and put a new paper washer in position on the joint face, after adding a light coat of jointing compound. Pressure from the pedal-return spring tends to push the operating plate away and it will greatly help the next stage of assembly if a piece of tubing is obtained (conduit tubing will be quite satisfactory) just small enough in diameter to pass through the operating plate bearing.

Take up the outer cover with the tube in position, and hold the operating plate against the spring pressure as the cover is located on its studs. Still holding the tube in position, manœuvre the kickstarter quadrant against its stop, check that the clutch operating lever is correctly positioned, and push the cover completely home.

It is essential that peg M in the outer cover is located between the tongues of the pedal-return spring on the carrier plate, otherwise the pedal will not return to its central position. Tighten all screws and nuts securely and then replace plungers O and E for the selector quadrant and the pawl plate. Replace the drain plug, and replenish with a recommended grade of lubricant, *see* page 4.

FOUR-SPEED GEARBOX C11G (1954–5). *To dismantle* the unit set the gears in the neutral position. Remove the drain plug and while the gearbox is draining, disconnect the speedometer and clutch cables. Release all the screws and nuts retaining the outer cover which is positioned by dowels and may require a sharp tap with a mallet to free it. The clutch operating lever will remain with the cover as it comes away, and also the gearchange lever with its selector arm O (*see* Fig. 38), and centralizing springs inside the cover. The kickstarter pedal, complete with internal quadrant and spring, will also be removed with the cover, but in this case, as the quadrant comes clear of its stop on the inner cover, the spring pressure on the pedal will be released suddenly. To avoid this, the clutch lever can be pulled out to its fullest extent allowing the kickstarter pedal to rest against it, so keeping the pressure under control. If it is required to replace the kickstarter spring first unhook it from the quadrant, then drive the cotter from the pedal, and remove the latter from its spindle. The quadrant is now free and can be removed. The spring is anchored by a small set-screw, with its locknut on the outside of the cover.

The speedometer-drive gear cannot be taken out until its bush is free, and this is held by a securing nut and a retaining pin on the outside of the cover. Take out the clutch push-rod (which passes through the centre of the mainshaft) and then dismantle the kickstarter ratchet assembly on the mainshaft. This is held by the nut on the end of the mainshaft, and it can be unscrewed (right-hand thread) after its locking washer has been straightened.

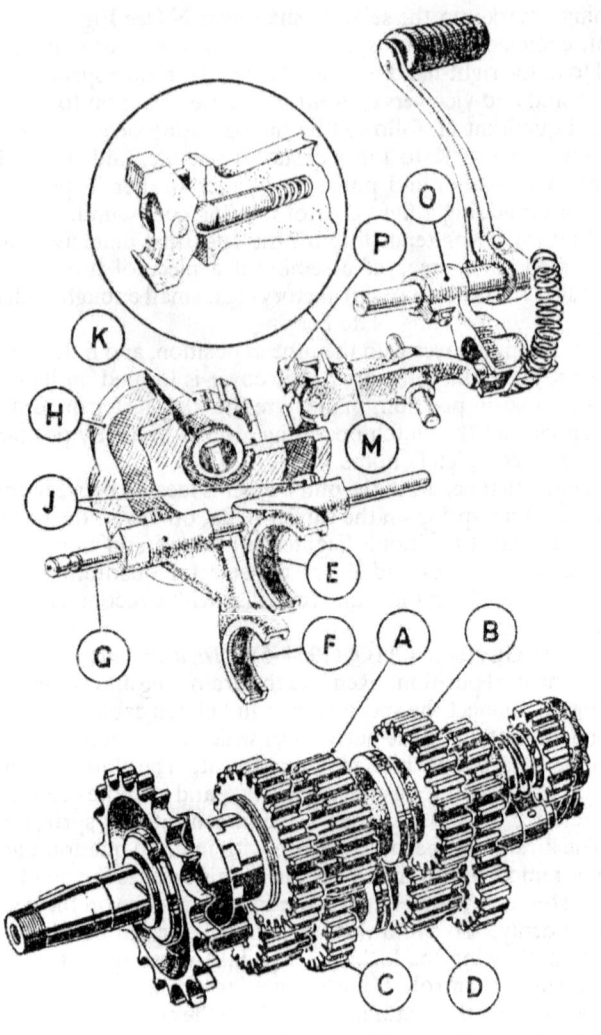

Fig. 38. Gear Cluster and Gear-change Mechanism in a Four-speed Gearbox

THE CLUTCH AND GEARBOX

The inner cover can now be withdrawn off its studs, carrying with it the gearchange rocking lever M. Its pivot pin is accessible when the gearchange spindle bush is pressed out of the cover, and a ¼ in. B.S.C. bolt can be used as an extractor for the pivot.

Selector fork shaft G is inserted into the end face of the gearbox and is secured by a grub-screw, which can be removed from below the box. Release the screw and pull out the shaft, leaving the two forks in position. The gear cluster, complete with mainshaft, layshaft, and the two forks, can be withdrawn bodily from the box, or they can be taken out individually. This is one of those tasks which is "easier said than done," but a little perseverance and a certain amount of manœuvring of components, will get the job done.

If the camplate H is to be removed, note first which notch is engaged by the control plunger, because this should be the neutral position which lies between first and second gears. It is important that the plunger is in this notch before the box is reassembled. Now unscrew the camplate plunger housing from the underside of the gearbox between the yoke plates, and remove the plunger assembly from the box. The camplate will now slide freely from its pivot. Both layshaft bushes are pressed into the gearbox shell and in the inner cover, and if they are to be replaced, can be driven out with the aid of a soft drift.

The pinion sleeve still remains in the gearbox and before this can be removed, the sprocket must be taken off. Straighten the lockwasher, then apply the rear brake and unscrew the sprocket locking ring. The sprocket can then be pulled off and the sleeve pinion tapped out of its bearing into the gearbox shell, using a wooden mallet. Next, disconnect the rear chain.

If the bearing is to be removed, first extract the circlip retaining the oil seal (on the outside of the bearing). Warm the shell and then drive out the bearing from inside the box.

Examination of the various parts will disclose which require renewal and amongst these, the following are worth special attention. If the selector forks show signs of heavy wear it is preferable to replace them rather than to attempt to erase any markings, as this will result in the creation of excessive side play and hence faulty gearchanges. The fixed pinions on both layshaft and mainshaft are pressed into position, and new components must be an equally tight fit. The camplate grooves must not be excessively worn, neither must the ratchet teeth on the back of the plate, nor the teeth on the selector claw P, as wear at any of these points can cause difficulty with gearchanging.

Reassembly. For the same reason as when removing the sleeve pinion bearing from the gearbox, warm the box when replacing it. Fit the bearing into the shell from the outside of the box as squarely as possible, to avoid jamming and so damaging the housing. In all probability the oilseal will require renewal and it must be fitted with its lipped face against the bearing, before its retaining circlip is put into position. The sleeve pinion can now be inserted into the bearing from inside the box. Replace the sprocket lockring with its washer and, after adding the rear chain, tighten the lockring securely. Be sure to bend the lock washer into one of the lockring grooves, to prevent it from working loose.

Now replace the camplate onto its pivot, and fit its control plunger into position from underneath the gearbox. Rotate the plate until the plunger locates in the neutral notch, which should have been specially noted when dismantling. Assemble the layshaft with selector fork F (*see* Fig. 38) fitting over the flanges of gears C and D, but leave the largest pinion on the bench for the moment. Slide the assembled layshaft into position in the box, and engage the fork peg in its track in the camplate H.

Next, assemble the mainshaft pinion onto the shaft, together with selector fork E, which fits over the flanges of gears A and B, and insert the complete assembly into the box, engaging the fork pegs J in their tracks on the camplate. The two forks should be approximately in line and their shaft can be gently passed through them, to the end of the gearbox, where it can be pressed home. Replace the shaft's grub-screw from below the box. Turning now to the layshaft, replace the thrust washer and the largest of the pinions, which is the last to be added.

Using a new paper washer between the shell of the box and the inner cover, this can be assembled next. Hold the gearchange rocking lever M in a central position, slide the cover onto the studs, and push home. The selector claw P must engage with the ratchet teeth K, on the back of the camplate.

The ratchet mechanism may now be fitted to the mainshaft, the washer being put on first, followed by the bush, spring, and ratchet pinion, the assembly being secured by the nut and its locking washer, which must be turned over the face of the nut, after tightening. Remember that this nut takes out all the end play from the mainshaft and must be securely tightened. Replace the clutch push-rod. The outer cover can be dealt with next. If the speedometer drive gear has been removed, this can be put back again, and locked in position by the retaining pin, after which its external nut can be tightened.

Replace the gearchange spindle with its selector arm O and centralizing springs. Add the gearchange pedal and tighten its clip bolt. Fit the kickstarter spring and quadrant in position, the eye of the spring being attached to the cover by its set-screw and nut, whilst its other end is hooked round the quadrant. Replace the kickstarter pedal and insert the cotter pin.

Place a new paper washer in position, and take up the cover with the kickstarter lever in the left hand, and the footchange lever in the right hand. Slide the cover onto its studs, turn the kickstarter lever a little, so that its quadrant will register with the ratchet pinion, and the gearchange selector arm with the ball on the end of the rocking lever. This may call for careful manipulation, because the speedometer drive gear must also engage with the pinion on the end of the layshaft.

Fasten all the nuts and screws round the cover. Drive the kickstarter pedal cotter pin firmly into position and replace the drain plug. Replenish the gearbox with a recommended grade of lubricant (*see* page 4).

THE CLUTCH AND GEARBOX 61

FOUR-SPEED GEARBOX 250 STAR. *Dismantling*—As the engine and gearbox are in unit construction on these models, the inner half of the primary chaincase is part of the crankcase and so cannot be removed. Once the clutch has been taken off the mainshaft (*see* "Removal and Replacement of the Clutch," page 46), a detachable plate registered in the back of the case is exposed. Take out the screws using the special screwdriver required for this purpose, and remove the plate with its oilseal, together with the felt washer specially provided for protection of the seal from grit. If the seal is to be renewed, remember that the new one must be fitted with its lip

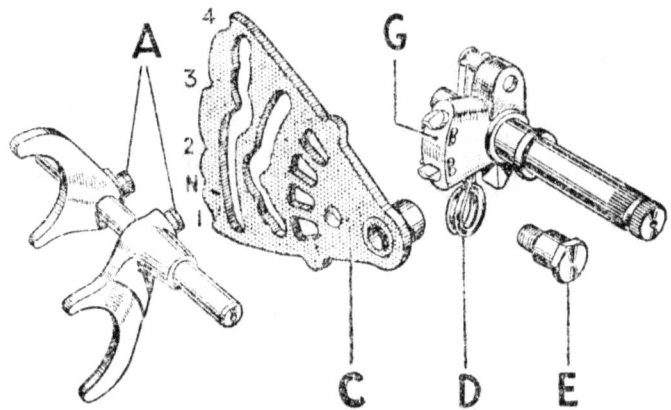

FIG. 39. GEAR-CHANGE MECHANISM IN THE 250 STAR, BARRACUDA AND STARFIRE GEARBOXES
(A pivot replaces bolt *E* after 1964)

facing the interior of the chaincase. The seal bears on an extension to the sleeve pinion bush and this must be in good condition otherwise it will quickly ruin the seal. If complete dismantling is to be carried out, the locking washer under the sprocket nut should first be straightened and the nut unscrewed, any tendency for this to rotate being counteracted by application of the rear brake. Disconnect the rear chain and pull the sprocket off the pinion sleeve.

Turning now to the offside of the gearbox, again because of the unit construction of the engine and gearbox, it will be necessary to remove both outer and inner timing covers, which necessitates exposing components which have no connexion with the gearbox. When the inner cover has been taken off, the valve timing gears will be visible, and therefore the dismantling process, so far, will be the same as that given for "Valve Timing" (*see* page 23). At this point, the gear cluster, shafts, and actuating mechanism, will be readily accessible.

Unscrew the spring pivot pin E (Fig. 39), which carries the gearchange pedal spring D, when the selector plunger quadrant G can be taken out of the box. This will allow the camplate to be lifted off the selector fork pegs A, and removed. On later models the quadrant plungers are retained by a small plate instead of by pins, but interchangeability is not affected.

The camplate spring B (*see* Fig. 40) can be detached if necessary, otherwise it can be left undisturbed. The whole of the gear cluster, together with the mainshaft, layshaft and selector forks can now be withdrawn, leaving the selector fork spindle and also the sleeve pinion (A) in the box.

Dismantling 250 Star (after 1964), Barracuda, and Starfire Models. The instructions given on page 27 for access to the valve timing gears, will allow the whole gearbox mechanism to be withdrawn. Then take out the selector

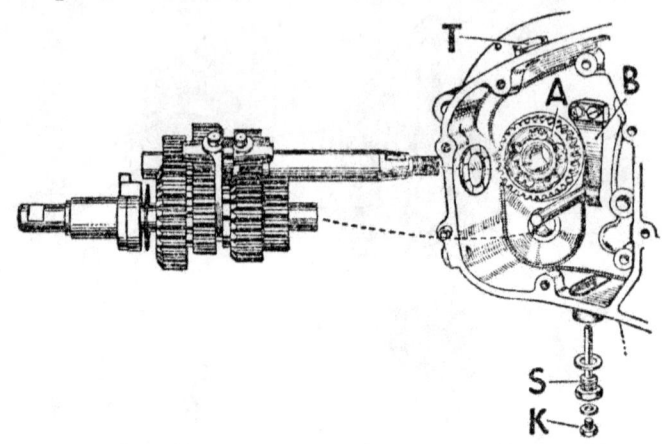

FIG. 40. GEAR CLUSTER OF THE 250 STAR GEARBOX

A quadrant-type starter mechanism is used on models manufactured after 1964 and a dipstick supersedes the level tube on the 1968 Starfire.

plunger quadrant and spring, but leave the spring pivot-bolt in position. Extract the split-pin from the cam-plate pivot and withdraw the latter. Now take out the cam-plate, together with the selector forks and spindle, the layshaft and loose gears. Note specially that the upper face of the cam-plate is marked "T" to ensure correct assembly. Worn cam-plate "windows" and/or quadrant plungers will cause poor gear changing and these items should be replaced if examination shows them to be faulty. The mainshaft can then be taken out for attention if required, following the removal of the locking nuts, ratchet mechanism, etc.

All Models—Whilst some of the gears will literally slide off their shafts, it should be noted that the smallest gear on the mainshaft has been pressed into position, and retains its adjacent gear. Similarly, the innermost gear on the layshaft is pressed on, also retaining its adjacent gear. To remove either of these gears, the shaft must be pressed out of both gears at the same time, necessitating the use of a hand press. On later models, including the Barracuda and Starfire gearboxes, the layshaft gear is integral with the shaft, its adjacent gear being retained by a circlip. The position of the various thrust washers should be specially noted because these may be slightly different in thickness and must be replaced in the same position from which they were removed.

If the sleeve pinion bearing is to be replaced, the bearing and sleeve can be removed together. Warm the gearbox shell around the bearing, in the manner already described, and tap the bearing into the box. The use of a tubular drift is advisable to avoid damage to the bush within the sleeve pinion and the oil-seal in front of the bearing. The seal can be drawn out once the bearing is out of the way and a replacement must be fitted with the lipped face to the inside of the gearbox. The bearing at the opposite end of the mainshaft is retained by a circlip.

Reassembly (*Models prior to* 1965). While the gearbox shell is still warm, a replacement bearing and/or sleeve pinion can be inserted and driven firmly home. It is essential for the bearing to be entered into its housing as squarely as possible to avoid jamming and perhaps damaging the gearbox. If it is the intention to replace one or more of the gears, an important point arises. After engine No. 24851, the tooth form of the gears was modified and therefore it will not be possible to replace one gear only. Its mating gear on the opposite shaft must also be changed, whether faulty or not.

Assemble the two shafts complete with the gear clusters, and the two selector forks as originally dismantled. The latter are interchangeable with each other, but it is preferable to replace them in their original positions. Make sure that their pegs and rollers are in good order.

Slide the whole assembly into position, feeding the selector forks onto their shaft as the assembly enters the box. When in position, refit the camplate onto the selector fork pegs, with the second-gear notch on the plate (Fig. 39), engaging with the spring blade at the back of the box. To facilitate the entry of the pegs into the grooves it may be necessary to manœuvre the gears a little, so that the forks move laterally on the shaft.

If the gearchange spring is to be replaced, hold the long stem of the quadrant shaft firmly (in a vice fitted with soft jaws) and, restraining the main loop with a tommy bar or similar tool, place a screwdriver between the tongues of the spring, twist to part them, and press over the shaft and its peg. The eye of the spring will appear twisted, but will be squared up as soon as the pivot pin is screwed home. Insert the quadrant shaft into its bush in the box, fit the eye-pin by hand, and as soon as it is correctly located, lock the bolt securely with a spanner.

In the absence of a jointing washer, smear a little jointing compound between the faces of the crankcase and inner cover, and feed the latter onto the various spindles, at the same time fitting the camplate into its slot. Fasten the cover to the crankcase (with the proper screwdriver for the job) and replace the camplate pivot. On no account forget its retaining pin. Add the small cover plate over the pivot, and to prevent oil leakage from this point, it is permissible to fit two $\frac{1}{16}$ in.-thick washers, as after engine No. 27665 a $\frac{1}{8}$ in.-thick washer was a standard fitment. Now temporarily replace the gearchange pedal and check the gear selection.

The kickstarter spring can be replaced next. Hook the inner end of the spring over the head of the screw which carries the kickstarter stop plate, and engage the tongue on the anchor plate with the outer end of the spring. The plate must be turned anti-clockwise through about 180 degrees until the flats in the hole and on the spindle register with each other, then press the plate into position. Pass the clutch cable through the back of the inner cover and couple to the clutch operating arm. While this is being done, take care to ensure that the ball is retained in the thrust plunger. A dab of grease will prove a great help.

The camshaft thrust washer is replaced with its countersunk face outwards. Remember to put the small peg into the shaft, and then the tag washer and nut. Tighten the nut firmly and secure it with the washer.

It now remains to fasten the outer cover in position, bearing in mind that the small-headed screw at the top of the cover is the locking screw for the contact-breaker unit. Unless extreme care has been taken, it will be most probable that the unit has moved a little from its original position, and although this will add more work to the operation just completed, it will be well worth while to check the ignition setting. The kickstarter cotter pin must be driven firmly into position, before tightening its nut.

Reassembly (250 Star, 1965–66). With the mainshaft in position in the inner cover, reassemble the gear cluster comprising layshaft, gears, and selector forks onto the mainshaft. The forks are interchangeable but should be replaced in their original positions. Now insert the selector-fork spindle through the forks and into its location in the cover. Slide the camplate through its slot in the cover, replace the pivot and do not forget to add the split pin.

Refit the camplate on to the fork pegs and position the plate so that when it is replaced, the second gear notch (Fig. 39) will engage with the spring plate at the back of the box.

Replacement of the selector quadrant spring requires care. With the short end uppermost, hold the shaft in a vice fitted with soft jaws and with the aid of two substantial levers (large screwdrivers will do) one placed between the prongs and the other through the loop, twist the spring until it slips over the short end of the shaft. Replace the quadrant in the cover and locate the spring over its pivot.

Reassembly 250 Star (1967), Barracuda and Starfire Models). Replace the cam-plate in its slot, insert the pivot pin and a new split-pin. Check that the letter "T" is uppermost on the plate. Replace the third-ratio pinion (plain bore) and the first-ratio pinion (splined bore) on the mainshaft and insert into the cover bearing. Hold the mainshaft firmly in a vice (using soft clamps to avoid damage), replace the kick-starter ratchet assembly and tighten the nut firmly, securing with the lock-washer.

At this point, lay the cover face downwards, place the layshaft shim, low ratio pinion (plain bore), and sliding third-ratio pinion (splined bore), in their correct positions on the cover, but without the layshaft. Add the layshaft selector fork, locating it in the lower track on the cam-plate.

The mainshaft second-ratio pinion (sliding) and spacers should next be fitted. Add its selector fork, locate it in the upper track on the cam-plate and pass the fork spindle through the forks and into the cover. Now replace the layshaft (with its two remaining pinions, circlip, etc., through the pinions which are already in position on the cover, and into its bearing on the kick-starter spindle.

Fit the gearchange quadrant assembly complete with spring into the cover, locating the spring eye over its pivot bolt. During this operation it will be necessary to depress the plungers with a strip of flat steel before they can be engaged in the cam-plate "windows" when the quadrant is pushed home. Now check the gear selection.

NOTE.—The thrust washer at the inner end of the layshaft should be of a thickness such that the end-float of the shaft is just perceptible. Spacers are also fitted on the mainshaft between pinions and spline ends, and their thicknesses must be adjusted to avoid excessive end-float of the pinions. Spacers of various thicknesses can be obtained from a B.S.A. Spares Stockist.

Star 250 (*after 1964*), *Barracuda and Starfire Models*. Add a little jointing compound to the faces of the crankcase and the inner cover, and carefully replace the latter, complete with gear cluster and gearchange mechanism. Satisfy yourself that everything is correctly located, and then firmly tighten the screws securing the cover to the crankcase. Now check the gear selection.

Insert the contact breaker into position and replace the central fixing bolt and mounting plate nuts loosely, because the ignition timing will have to be re-set later (*see* page 19). Replace the starter spindle, spring and bush.

If the clutch operating mechanism has been disturbed, replace the "rack" type plunger and ball in the cover, insert the actuating lever through the top of the cover, and engage the pinion with the rack on the plunger. To replace the starter spring is quite simple. Locate the hooked end of the spring into its slot on the starter quadrant. Then turn the body of the spring in a clockwise direction until the "eye" of the opposite end of the spring can be fitted on to its stud.

Re-fit the outer cover, taking care not to damage the oil seal at the starter spindle, and couple up the clutch cable, followed by replacement of the starter and gearchange pedals. The clutch-cable adjustment is described on page 43. The ignition timing must be re-set in accordance with the details given on page 19.

All models—Now attend to the nearside of the gearbox. Details have already been given of the removal of the gearbox sprocket, felt washer, etc., and when replacing, the essential point is to tighten the sprocket locknut securely and to lock it with the tab washer. Refit the circular cover complete with its seal, and add a new paper washer. Replace the clutch push-rod.

With the assembly of the gearbox completed, the next stage is the replacement of the clutch, primary drive, and the alternator of which details have already been given.

4 Decarbonizing the Engine

BEFORE starting to decarbonize the engine there are one or two special tools that will be required. A valve spring compression tool will prove a useful acquisition, and when dealing with an O.H.V. engine, a suction-type valve grinding tool will be necessary as the valve heads are not provided with a slot for the reception of a screwdriver blade. Grinding paste, suitable brushes, paraffin, a tube of jointing compound and a set of gaskets will also be required. All these items can be obtained through any B.S.A. dealer.

Preliminary Work. The S.V. model is the only one with sufficient space between the cylinder head and the petrol tank, for the work to be carried out in comfort with the tank in position, and on all other models it must be taken off. It is not necessary to drain the tank, if the tap is turned off and the pipe disconnected just below the tap. In some cases, the pipe has a screw connexion and in others the pipe is a push-fit direct onto the tap. On Model, C11G and C12 the tank is attached to the frame at the steering head, and to the frame top at the rear. Rubber mountings are used at this point, their fixing bolts being wired together to prevent accidental loss. The tanks on the 250 Star, Barracuda and Starfire are mounted on rubber pads below the front and rear, and are clamped by means of the central bolt concealed by the rubber cap. Note carefully the order of dismantling, as the mountings are designed so that there is no direct contact between tank and frame.

The engine steady (complete with exhaust-valve lifter assembly in the case of the earlier Barracuda and Starfire) between the cylinder head and the frame tube can be removed next. The exhaust pipe is a push-fit in the cylinder head, but it may require a tap with a mallet to release it, due to carbon deposit round the pipe. The 250 Star, Barracuda, and Starfire are fitted with a finned collar at this point, and it also must be released before the pipe can be removed. Now uncouple the oil feed to the rockers (not fitted to earlier C11G engines). A rubber sleeve connects the carburettor to the air cleaner on the 250 Star, and this must be disconnected before the carburettor can be drawn off its studs. On other models, where an air cleaner is fitted, it can be unscrewed from the carburettor intake.

There is no necessity to dismantle the carburettor, as it can be left attached to its control cables, and tied back out of the way.

Unscrew the sparking plug, and rotate the engine until the piston is at the top dead centre, i.e. with both valves closed. In this position the rocker mechanism will be relieved of pressure from the valve springs.

DECARBONIZING THE ENGINE

Removing the Cylinder Head. On the S.V. engine the cylinder head is freed for removal, simply by unscrewing the holding-down bolts.

C11G AND C12 ENGINES. It only requires removal of the central bolt in order to take off the rocker cover. Examine the joint washer for signs of oil leakage, and if necessary replace with a new one when reassembling. The nuts retaining the cylinder head are located between the fins at the sides of the barrel, and when these have been removed, raise the head from the barrel by an amount sufficient to enable the push-rods to be freed from the rockers and withdraw the rods. The head, complete with its fixing studs, can now be lifted off, but if it shows some tendency to stick, a few light taps with a mallet under the exhaust port will loosen it.

250 STAR. Long studs hold the rocker box to the head, and as there is insufficient clearance between the box and the frame tube, the head must be taken off with the rocker box still in position. Four nuts hold the head to the barrel on studs which pass through the cylinder fins into the crankcase. To take off the head, raise it sufficiently to clear the studs, rotate it round the push-rod tube through 180 degrees so as to clear the frame, and lift off. Take the push-rods out of the tube, and then remove the latter together with the sealing rings at both ends. These are made of a special heat- and oil-resisting rubber and any replacements must be of the same material.

The rocker box can now be detached from the head, seven of its nuts being of the self-locking type, and the three inspection covers removed. If the box is to be wholly dismantled, the rocker spindles can be driven out from the threaded end with a copper drift, and a note kept of the sequence of assembly of the thrust washers, etc. A small sealing ring is fitted to each spindle, and great care must be exercised when re-inserting the spindle into the rocker box to avoid damage to the seal.

BARRACUDA AND STARFIRE ENGINES. Similar instructions to those for the 250 Star apply to these two engines, except that six nuts retain the cylinder head, and the push-rod tube is integral with the barrel. An exhaust-valve lifter is incorporated in the rocker-box on earlier models, but unless it is suspected of being faulty, it need not be disturbed. There are no sealing rings for the rocker spindles.

The Cylinder Head Gasket. This should be clean and bright all over: dark patches indicate that it has been "blowing." Signs of burning, particularly round the cylinder bore, will be self-evident and with either of these faults, a new gasket must be fitted. On the C11G and C12 engines the special lay out of the push-rods requires offset holes in the gasket, and any replacement must be positioned correctly. In addition to the four stud holes in the gasket for the 250 Star, four smaller holes will be noticed and these coincide with oil drainage holes in the head and barrel. Obviously, the gasket must be replaced so that these holes coincide, otherwise the oil return from the rocker box will be interrupted. Six stud holes in the gasket used on the Barracuda and Starfire engines prevent the possibility of misalignment of the oil holes.

Removal of the Valves. The use of a valve removal tool, which is the same in principle for both the S.V. and O.H.V. engines is shown in Fig. 41. A B.S.A. service tool, suitable for all engines, is available under Part No. 61–3340, and can be obtained through any B.S.A. spares stockist. Screw up the wing nut until the spring and its collar are compressed sufficiently for the split collets to become accessible. With their removal, unscrew the wing nut until the spring has expanded to its free length, and take out the spring(s), collar, and valve. The inlet and exhaust valves are made of different materials because of the different temperatures they have

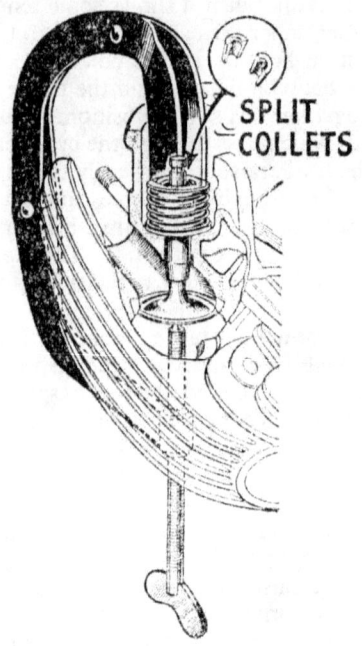

Fig. 41. Valve Spring Compressor in use on O.H.V. Engine

to withstand, and on these engines, where the valves are the same size, it is important that some distinguishing mark should be made on them, so that they can be replaced on the same seat from which they were removed.

Decarbonizing. It is preferable to leave the barrel in position for the time being, as it supports the piston and leaves both hands free for decarbonizing. Rotate the engine so that the piston is at the top of its stroke, and carefully scrape all the carbon off the piston crown with the aid of a blunt tool such as an old screwdriver. This is a job requiring a little patience in order to avoid scoring the soft aluminium surface of the piston.

Also scrape the carbon from the ports in the cylinder head and in the combustion chamber, which in the case of the 250 Star, Barracuda and

DECARBONIZING THE ENGINE

Starfire engines, is of aluminium with cast-iron valve seats. Here, too, scoring of the combustion chamber particularly, must be avoided.

The ports in the S.V. engine are, of course, in the cylinder barrel and with this model it will be easier to decarbonize the ports if the barrel is taken off the crankcase. Remove all traces of loose carbon and dust.

Replacing the Valve Guides. Worn guides can be driven out by means of a suitable punch from inside the port. A piece of $\frac{7}{16}$ in. rod turned down at one end to fit into the guide, makes an admirable tool for this job.

New guides, which must be a tight fit in the head or barrel, are driven into position from above. Parallel guides are used on the C10L engine, and they must be fitted so that the inlet guide is $1\frac{1}{16}$ in. from the top face of the cylinder barrel, and the exhaust guide is $1\frac{3}{8}$ in. from the same face. Note that the exhaust guide is counterbored for a short distance at one end and this end must be uppermost.

The guides on the C11G and C12 engines are flanged and must be driven in as far as possible. The flange also serves to retain the lower spring collar against the cylinder head.

A circlip is fitted to the valve guides on the 250 Star to determine their position in the cylinder head, but in this case the spring collar is loose and can be fitted afterwards. Double-diameter valve guides are used on the Barracuda and Starfire engines. Note that the exhaust guide is counter bored at the end protruding into the port.

With new guides fitted in the head or barrel, the valve seats must be re-faced with a proper cutter (*see* Fig. 42) to ensure concentricity of the seat and guide, and this work is best carried out by a B.S.A. dealer.

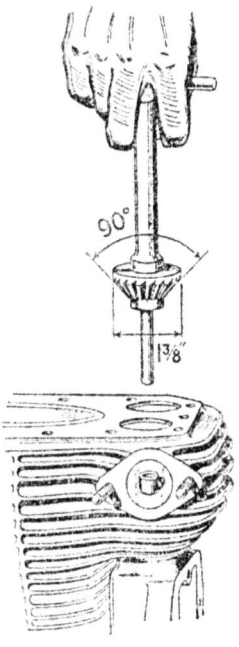

FIG. 42. RECUTTING THE VALVE SEATS

Alternatively, for those who wish to carry out this work themselves, B.S.A. service tools are available under the following Part Nos. 61–3293 and 61–3300 (250 Star, Barracuda and Starfire); and 61–3298, 61–3293, and 61–3290 for all other models.

Examination of Valves and Seats. If the valve faces show considerable evidence of "pitting" (i.e. deeply pock-marked), no attempt should be made to grind the valves by hand until the face has been restored by grinding on a machine specially made for this purpose. Such work can usually be undertaken by most B.S.A. dealers or garages. If grinding by hand is attempted, in these circumstances, it is most likely that too much material will be removed from the seats in the cylinder head or barrel, resulting in "pocketing" of the valve, and hence reduced performance. This point is very important when the cylinder head is of aluminium, with the special inserts cast in position, and which cannot be replaced. Should the pitting be extremely deep, restoring the face may result in a sharp edge to the valve head, in which case the valve must be replaced by a new one. Similarly, if the edge of the valve head shows signs of burning away at the edges, it should be replaced without hesitation.

Alternatively, if the valve face and seats in the head or barrel are only lightly pitted or perhaps only discoloured, then hand grinding with fine paste will be sufficient.

The valve faces are usually the first to become pitted, the seats in the head or barrel remaining in a reasonable condition, but if they, too, are pitted the head or barrel should be taken to a B.S.A. dealer for re-facing with a proper seating-cutter (*see* Fig. 42).

Clean all the carbon from the top and the underside of the valve head. Also examine the stem and if badly worn, replace the valve, because accurate seating will be unlikely and may also lead to other difficulties after reassembly.

Valve Springs. These operate under extremely arduous conditions at high temperatures and as a result tend to lose their efficiency after a considerable mileage has been covered. The free lengths of the springs can be compared with those given below, and if there is an appreciable difference, the springs should be renewed. New spring lengths are as follows— C10L—2 in.; C11G, C12,—2 in. and $1\frac{11}{16}$ in.; 250 Star and Competition model—$2\frac{1}{32}$ and $1\frac{5}{8}$ in.; 250 Star SS80 and Scrambles model—1·67 in. and 1·50 in.; Barracuda and Starfire—$1\frac{3}{4}$ in. and $1\frac{7}{16}$ in.

Grinding-in the Valves. Fine grinding paste will be satisfactory for use with valves which are in reasonable condition or which have been re-faced. Valves which are in poor condition but not bad enough to warrant re-facing by machine, should first be ground with the coarse grade of paste, finishing off with the fine.

Use only a small quantity of paste and remember to replace the valve on the same seat from which it was removed. The special grinding tool shown in Fig. 43 adheres to the valve head by suction and enables the valve to be rotated backwards and forwards while maintaining a steady pressure. The suction disc should be slightly damped. A light spring placed under the head of the valve will assist in raising the head periodically so that it can be turned to a new position and the grinding process continued until the mating surfaces of the valve and seat show a uniform matt surface all the way round. Wash the valve and seat thoroughly in paraffin to remove all traces of grinding paste which can be extremely harmful if it finds its way into the engine.

Replacing the Valves. First make sure that all traces of valve-grinding compound have been removed and that the lower spring collar is against

DECARBONIZING THE ENGINE

the cylinder head (not fitted on C10L engines). Oil the stem and replace the valve. Add the spring and collar over the exposed stem and, using the spring-compressing tool, close the spring until the split collets can be inserted in the stem recess. A dab of grease in the recess will retain the collets while the spring is being released. Before removing the tool check that the collets are properly seated in the recess.

Note. The collets, collars, etc., for the 1969/70 Starfire engines differ in angle from those used in previous, years and hence are not interchangeable.

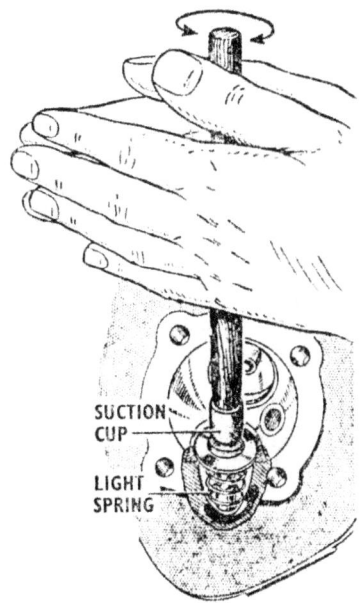

FIG. 43. SPECIAL TOOL FOR GRINDING-IN THE VALVES ON O.H.V. ENGINES

Reassembling the Head. Once the valves and springs are in position there should be little or no difficulty with the reassembly of the head. If the rockers on the C12 and C11G engines have been taken off their spindles, the most important point to remember when replacing them is to fit the split pin after the thrust washer and nut have been added.

With the 250 Star, it has already been mentioned that the oil sealing ring on the rocker spindles must be protected from damage when reinserting the spindle, and the various thrust washers must be assembled in the correct order. Refit the assembled rocker-box on to the head, using a new gasket smeared with jointing compound, and tighten down with the self-locking nuts on all studs except those for the engine steady mounting. There is no need to replace the three inspection covers at this stage, as the tappets will have to be reset, and the push-rods fitted to the rocker pins later.

Removing the Cylinder Barrel. C10L ENGINE. Five nuts and studs hold the barrel to the crankcase. Four of these are visible round the base flange of the barrel, but the fifth is inside the tappet chest between the tappets, and it is necessary to take off the tappet cover before the nut becomes accessible. Rotate the engine gently until the piston is at the bottom of its stroke and lift the barrel up, at the same time tilting it forwards.

As the piston emerges from the barrel it should be supported so as to prevent possible damage to the skirt by contact with the crankcase or connecting-rod. As a precaution against the entry of foreign matter into the crankcase, cover the mouth with a piece of cloth.

C11G AND C12 ENGINES. The cylinder barrel on these engines is removed in the same way as for the C10L, but as these are O.H.V. engines there are six nuts round the flange of the barrel. As with the cylinder-head gasket, the paper washer between the barrel and the crankcase is pierced with offset holes to clear the push-rods and a new washer must be replaced the correct way round.

250 STAR, BARRACUDA AND STARFIRE ENGINES. Rotate the engine until the piston is at the bottom of its stroke and slide the barrel upwards over its studs, steadying the piston as it emerges from the barrel to prevent it becoming damaged. The barrel is deeply registered into the crankcase and it may be found necessary to slacken the two crankcase bolts just below the barrel. The paper washer at the joint face is almost certain to require renewal, and special care must be taken to ensure that the small oil holes correspond with similar holes in the barrel and crankcase, otherwise the oil return from the rocker-box will be obstructed.

Examination of the Cylinder Bore. Should the bore be worn it will show itself by the formation of a ridge a short distance from the top face and it will be advisable to have the barrel rebored. This will also be necessary if there are any deep score marks in the wall of the cylinder, as these will cause excessive oil consumption and loss of compression.

The Piston. As a rule it is not necessary to remove the piston and rings until the machine has covered a considerable mileage, but if excessive piston tap is in evidence when the engine is hot, or the oil consumption is exceptionally heavy, this may indicate that either the piston or the rings require attention.

The gudgeon-pin is retained at each end by a small circlip, and one of these must be extracted by the use of a pointed instrument such as a steel knitting needle. To help in removal of the gudgeon-pin, it is a good idea to warm the aluminium piston, and a simple way of doing this is to stand an electric iron on the crown, when the heat will flow through the walls of the piston to the gudgeon-pin bosses, expanding them slightly. When the piston is thoroughly warm, tap out the gudgeon-pin with a hammer and copper drift of a size slightly smaller than the pin diameter. It is essential for the piston to be supported on the opposite side while carrying out this operation in order to avoid any side loading on the connecting-rod. Mark the inside wall of the piston for identification purposes, so that it can be replaced the same way round.

When refitting, warm the piston as previously mentioned, smear engine oil on the gudgeon-pin and tap into position, again supporting the piston as this is done. It is most important that the circlip be refitted in the groove in the piston boss, as if this is omitted, the gudgeon-pin may move and badly score the cylinder walls.

The Piston Rings. All the rings must be quite free in their grooves but with a minimum of up-and-down play, and if stuck, they must be prised

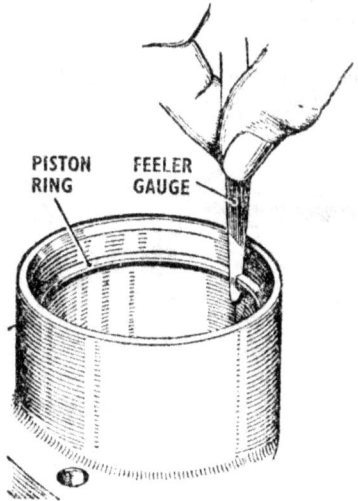

Fig. 44. Checking Piston Ring Gaps
Each ring in turn should be pushed squarely into the barrel using a piston for the purpose.

out as carefully as possible. To avoid the possibility of breaking the rings when removing them from the piston, three strips of brass, about ¼ in. wide by 3 in. long should be used. Taking the lowest ring first, place the strips, one at a time, between the ring and the piston, working them round the piston so that they lie equidistant round it. The ring can now be gently slid off, but a tendency for the ring to hug the piston near the gap should be watched.

The contact face of the rings should be of a uniformly matt finish all the way round and if bright patches or discoloration are evident, the rings must be replaced. In addition, the joint gap must not be excessive. The ends of the rings will spring apart appreciably when free from restraint and to test the gap under working conditions place the ring in the lower end of the cylinder bore (where the least wear has taken place), pushing it in squarely by means of the piston, and check the gap with a feeler gauge (*see* Fig. 44). The recommended gap for new rings is 0·009–0·013 in. and if this figure is considerably exceeded then new rings must be fitted.

To give a greater degree of oil control on the 250 Star, the second compression ring (centre groove) was changed in mid-season to the taper type, and it is essential that this ring is fitted with the correct face uppermost. The taper is extremely slight and to avoid confusion the top face is marked with a letter T. The taper compression ring was introduced on the 250 Star at engine No. 24401, the Trials model at engine No. 1182, and the Scrambles Model at engine No. 2171, and as it is interchangeable with the plain compression ring it can be fitted to any machine on which the oil consumption is regarded as excessive. All Barracuda and Starfire engines are fitted with a taper second compression ring.

The Connecting-rod Little-end. While the piston is dismantled, examine the bore of the little-end bearing and check the fit of the gudgeon-pin. This

FIG. 45. DRAW-BOLT EXTRACTOR FOR REMOVING THE LITTLE-END BUSH
The same tool can be used when replacing the bush.

should be such that when there is a smear of oil on the pin, it should slide freely into the bush without play. The amount by which the gudgeon-pin itself has worn can usually be felt with the fingers and unless the surface is smooth and free from ridges, a new pin is necessary. Fit this into the little-end bush and if there is still play present, a new bush is required. This can be fitted without dismantling the connecting-rod if a suitable extractor is used as shown in Fig. 45. An extractor can be provided by a B.S.A. Spares Stockist under the following part numbers: C10L, C11G and C12—No. 61-3656, 250 Star—No. 61-3659; Barracuda and Starfire—No. 61-3794. The extractor is so constructed that tightening of the bolt head draws the washer along the bolt pushing the bush before it into the extension sleeve. A new bush can be inserted with the same tool, and as the bush will close a little when being pressed home it must be reamed accurately to size when in position. An important point to remember when inserting the bush is that oil holes (if any) must be correctly aligned with each other. The reamer sizes are as follows: C10L, C11G and C12 ⅜ in., 250 Star, Barracuda and Starfire—⅝ in.

The Connecting-rod Big-end. At this stage of dismantling the engine it is not possible to renew any of the big-end components as this means removing the engine from its frame, but it is a good opportunity of checking the big-end for wear. There should not be any direct up and down movement of the rod but the big-end is permitted a little sideways movement and this will allow corresponding movement of the little-end. Also, the running clearance of the big-end will allow a trace of sideways rock at the little-end.

If the big-end is worn and a new one is to be fitted, then the engine must be removed (*see* Chapter 5).

Notes on Engine Reassembly. Before commencing reassembly, all parts must be thoroughly washed in paraffin, dried, and lubricated with engine oil on all working surfaces.

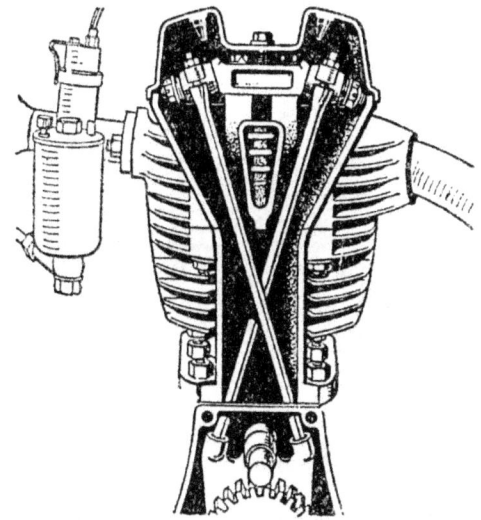

FIG. 46. POSITIONING THE PUSH-RODS ON THE O.H.V. C12 ENGINE

Assuming that the piston and rings have been replaced on the connecting-rod as described in a previous section, turn the rings so that their joints are equally spaced round the piston, and place a new paper washer in position on the crankcase face. Now slide the barrel over the piston, holding the barrel with one hand while compressing the rings with the other. Each ring should be compressed in turn so that it will enter the mouth of the barrel at approximately the correct size. A chamfer is provided at the base of the cylinder bore to act as a "lead-in" for the rings, but it is all too easy to trap the ring during this part of the assembly. The job is rendered much easier and safer if a compressor band is used. B.S.A. Service tool No. 61-3682 is available for this purpose and is suitable for the 250 Star, Barracuda, and Starfire engines. Other engines require tool No. 61-5051. It will be found that the barrel will push the band down as each successive ring passes into it.

C10L ENGINE. The valves will already have been refitted to the barrel and the engine should now be rotated so that the tappets are in their lowest position, otherwise the pressure of the valve springs will prevent the barrel from seating properly. Tighten the nuts firmly, each one a little at a time to avoid distortion of the base flange. Remember that there are five of these nuts in all, one being inside the tappet chest. The cylinder head and gasket

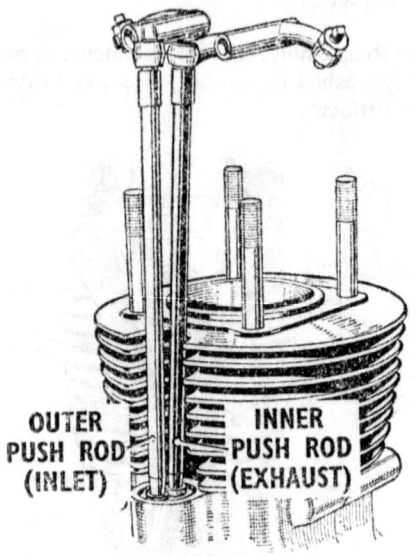

FIG. 47. POSITIONING THE PUSH-RODS ON THE 250 STAR, BARRACUDA AND STARFIRE ENGINES

are held by eight bolts and these should be tightened lightly at first and then a quarter of a turn at a time, working in diagonal order, i.e. when a bolt has been tightened the next one to receive attention is on the opposite side of the head and *not* the one next to it. One bolt only has an extension for mounting the engine steady and must be replaced in the correct position at the front of the head.

C11G AND C12 ENGINES. In the section on removing the cylinder barrel, the importance of fitting the cylinder base washer the correct way round was emphasized, and this also applies to the cylinder head gasket. If these are incorrectly fitted, the push-rods cannot be replaced and the engine will have to be dismantled again. When the barrel is tightened down to the crankcase, the piston should be set at the top of its compression

DECARBONIZING THE ENGINE

stroke and the assembled head put loosely in position. Before the head is fastened down, ease it up a little and insert the push-rods into their appropriate apertures, the plain end of each rod fitting into the cup formed in the cam follower in the crankcase, and the cupped end of the rod locating in the ball pin on the end of the rocker arm. It is most important to note on these engines that the push-rods are crossed (*see* Fig. 46), and that to facilitate assembly the exhaust rod must be fitted first. Now tighten the seven cylinder head nuts following the procedure adopted for the C10L engine.

250 STAR ENGINES. On these engines the cylinder head clamps the barrel to the crankcase so that following replacement of the barrel, the push-rod tube should next be set in position. Note that the sealing washers at the top and bottom of the tube are of special material and normal rubber is unsuitable as a replacement. Now insert the two push-rods into the tube, fitting their lower plain ends into the cupped ends of the tappets.

The assembled cylinder head can be refitted and here it must be remembered that the head must be placed over the push-rods but at 180 degrees to its normal position, then swung into its correct place, and lowered onto the cylinder studs. Through the inspection aperture in the rocker box, fit the cupped ends of the push-rods into the ball pins on the rocker arms. The lower end of the push-rod on the outside of the engine fits into the inlet rocker (*see* Fig. 47), the exhaust rod being on the inside. Tighten the cylinder nuts lightly at first and then a quarter of a turn at a time in diagonal order, i.e. at opposite corners in turn.

BARRACUDA AND STARFIRE ENGINES. The details given for the 250 Star apply to these engines except that the push rod tube is integral with the barrel.

General. Do not hesitate to renew all or any of the gaskets or paper washers if there is any doubt about their efficiency and in particular to clean the metal surface before the washers are fitted. The carburettor flange washer or rubber "O" ring must be in good order otherwise an air leakage is likely to interfere with carburation, and when replacing the carburettor take great care with the insertion of the air slide and the needle, as the latter is easily bent.

As the valves have been ground in, the valve clearances will have been disturbed and it will be necessary to reset them in accordance with the instructions on page 11.

The fitting of the remaining items, namely engine steady, exhaust system, petrol tank, etc., should not present any particular difficulties.

5 Dismantling and Reassembly of the Engine

To remove the engine from the frame and dismantle it entirely is a major job especially if it is carried out single-handed, but provided that much of the engine and its auxiliaries are dismantled in position, the task becomes much easier, if only because of the fact that the crankcase is considerably lighter to handle than a complete engine.

Most of the preliminary work has already been dealt with in other chapters, leaving the main work connected with the stripping and re-assembly of the crankcase. For example, the chapter on decarbonizing explains how to strip the engine down to the crankcase face, and removal of the primary drive and clutch are dealt with under "Access to the Clutch," page 43. In the case of the 250 Star, Barracuda and Starfire models, removal of the clutch automatically includes removal of the alternator, but on other models this is a separate operation, and is necessary in order to allow the back of the chaincase to be taken off.

With this exception, therefore, it will be assumed that only the crankcase remains in the frame, and is ready for removal and dismantling.

C10L, C11G, C12 ENGINES

Disconnect the alternator leads at their snap connectors outside the chaincase, and make a careful note of the positions and colours of the various cables for reassembly purposes. The rotor of the alternator is retained on the mainshaft by a nut and locking washer, and these must be removed next. Take off the stator nuts (either three or four according to the age of the machine) and draw the stator off its studs. A chamfer is provided at the back of the alternator housing, so that a screwdriver can be inserted if necessary, and the stator and its housing gently prised free. Next, pull the rotor off the mainshaft (take care not to lose the key), followed by the "dished" washer and the engine sprocket. The alternator housing is held to the crankcase by a single bolt, and after its removal the housing and spacer sleeves can be withdrawn. On models employing four studs, the housing is retained by two nuts. A variant of this assembly is that of a brass shield behind the stator used in conjunction with a plain steel one on the mainshaft, both of which were superseded at a later date by the "dished" washer previously mentioned.

Remove the back half of the primary chaincase. Take off the contact-breaker cover and disconnect the lead from its terminal (*see* Figs. 9 and 10), so that the lead can be passed through the grommet in the gearbox shield when the latter has been released.

DISMANTLING AND REASSEMBLY OF THE ENGINE

Drain the tank, and disconnect the pipes at their unions on the crankcase. The front yoke plates (engine to frame) can now be taken off, but before releasing the rear of the crankcase, slacken the bolts clamping the yoke plates to the gearbox and to the frame, as these plates also grip the crankcase lugs. Now take out the remaining crankcase securing studs and lift out the crankcase.

Crankcase Dismantling. Remove the contact-breaker, auto-advance mechanism and the timing cover to expose the timing gears. This sequence is detailed on page 23 in the section dealing with valve timing.

The camshaft can be pulled out of its bearing in the crankcase, and after

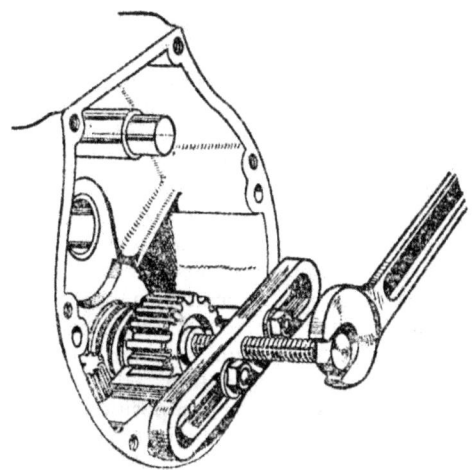

FIG. 48. WITHDRAWING THE ENGINE MAINSHAFT PINION (C10L, C11G AND C12 ENGINES)

extracting the circlip, the cam followers and spacing sleeve can be drawn off their shaft, which is pressed into the case and need not be disturbed.

The mainshaft pinion, in addition to being held in position by a nut locked with a tag washer, is also a tight fit on the shaft and is keyed to it. An extractor will be required to move this pinion, and Fig. 48 shows how it should be used. The extractor Part No. is 61–3678 and is used in conjunction with jaws Part No. 61–1733. The worm, which is integral with the mainshaft pinion, drives the oil-pump spindle and the latter cannot be lifted out until its locating pin is extracted. This is tapped to take one of the timing cover screws, and after it has been inserted the pin can be withdrawn from the crankcase and the spindle taken out upwards into the timing case. The pin is sometimes covered with a washer, which must be removed before the screw can be inserted.

Turning now to the drive-side of the case, remove any shims which may have been fitted behind the sprocket to give correct chain alignment, and then the drilled sleeve which passes through the oil-seal and abuts the mainshaft ballrace. The sleeve is actually a "breathing" device, and carries a location peg to ensure correct timing.

The crankcase halves are joined together by six studs, four of which can be removed completely, and two at the mouth of the crankcase which are fixed in the timing-side half. Take off all the nuts and the crankcase is ready for separating.

The timing side registers in the driving side and if jointing compound has been used during the previous assembly, a few careful blows with a soft mallet may be required to enable the halves to be separated. Once the joint faces are separated, the timing side (which incorporates a plain bearing) can be drawn off the mainshaft, leaving the flywheel and mainshaft assembly in the driving-side of the case. Two items still remain in the timing side. The non-return valve in the delivery oil-way can be taken out (*see* page 6), and removal of the cover plate and filter below the case will expose the oil pump. This should not be removed unless it is known to be at fault, in which case its two retaining bolts (identified by spring washers beneath their heads) must be removed.

Reverting to the drive-side of the case, the mainshaft will probably be a tight fit in the ballrace, in which case some assistance will be required.

Hold the crankcase just above the bench with the driveside mainshaft uppermost, so that an assistant can strike the end of the mainshaft with a lead hammer, driving it through the bearing to the inside of the case. This is a job requiring care and patience to avoid damage, and as the flywheels may be released suddenly, they should be poised at a minimum distance above the bench throughout this operation.

The ballrace and oil-seal will still be in position and if these are to be renewed, first prise out the ballrace-retaining circlip. Heat the case in hot water and drive out the bearing with a suitable punch applied from the outside of the case. While the case is still warm, refit the new bearing complete with its inner oil-retaining washer, using a tubular punch on the outer ring of the bearing, and return the circlip to its groove. If the oil-seal is to be replaced, it must be inserted so that its lip faces the inside of the case.

Plain bearings in the timing side of the crankcase and the timing cover can be renewed easily if the latter is first heated in hot water. The new bushes should be reamed to size after fitting, but special attention is necessary in the case of a new mainshaft bush to ensure accurate alignment of the mainshafts. The crankcase halves must be temporarily bolted together for the operation, and a special reamer (B.S.A. service tool Part No. 61-1932) is available for the job, but as it is an expensive item it will be as well to have the work carried out by a B.S.A. dealer.

Dismantling the flywheels and fitting a new big-end bearing is a matter for a B.S.A. dealer, because of the equipment required not only in dismantling and reassembly, but also in truing the flywheels afterwards. However, for those who wish to attempt this work themselves, the following notes will prove to be of use, but it will still be necessary to make a certain amount of equipment and possibly borrow the remainder.

DISMANTLING AND REASSEMBLY OF THE ENGINE 81

Dismantling the Big-end. The crankcase assembly must be held securely so as to leave both hands free for releasing the crankpin nuts. Two ⅜ in. posts should be fixed rigidly to the bench with their centres precisely 3⅞ in. apart, and midway between them bore a hole of at least 1 in. diameter.

Mount the flywheels so that the mainshaft passes through the hole, and the posts through the two holes in the flywheels. Now apply a box-spanner to the crankpin nut, using a tommy-bar extending about 12 in. on each side of the spanner, so that both hands can be used to obtain adequate leverage.

The crankpin fits into taper holes in the flywheels and can be released by means of a sharp blow at each end with a mallet. In the timing-side flywheel, the crankpin carries a key in order to ensure correct relationship of the oil holes when the flywheels are assembled.

Big-end assemblies can be obtained as complete units, and owners are strongly advised to take advantage of this fact and not to attempt to make-do with such expedients as the fitting of oversize rollers. A new big-end is built by selective assembly methods, as the clearances are critical, and such an assembly comprises the connecting-rod, rollers and crankpin, which can be obtained ready for immediate fitting.

Reassembling the Big-end. All components must be clean and free from foreign matter, and the bearing coated with engine oil. In particular, the crankpin and flywheel tapers must be absolutely clean and dry. Fit the flywheels to the new crankpin, remembering to put the key in the crankpin on the timing side, and lightly tighten the nuts. The rig that was made for dismantling can now be used for the preliminary tightening of the nuts. Place the flywheels over the posts, tighten the timing-side crankpin nut first, very firmly indeed, until the crankpin collar seats against the flywheel face, and check with a feeler gauge that this condition has been attained. Punch the edge of the crankpin with a centre punch to lock the nut. At the same time rivet over the grub-screw in the end of the crankpin. This screw seals the oilfeed to the big-end and if lost, the engine will be seriously damaged.

Reverse the whole assembly so that the driving side is uppermost and tighten the crankpin nut firmly, but not yet finally. This is the first stage in aligning the flywheels and mainshaft. The next step is to fit the ballrace on to the drive-side mainshaft, not forgetting the oil-retaining washer between the race and flywheel. A similar bearing is added temporarily on the timing-shaft side, and the whole assembly mounted in vee blocks. The faces and rims of the flywheels must run true to within 0·005 in. and for this purpose a dial gauge or similar instrument (*see* Fig. 49) will be necessary, in order to locate the high spots. Correction should be made by means of light blows with a lead hammer. When the mis-alignment does not exceed 0·005 in. fully tighten the drive-side crankpin nut. With the crankpin fully home in both flywheels, the side clearance between the connecting-rod and flywheels should not be less than 0·009 in. nor greater than 0·013 in.

The third stage consists in truing the wheels to within a maximum figure of 0·002 in. The lead hammer, again used on the wheels only and never on the shafts, will provide a sufficiently heavy blow for the final truing. Take the bearings off the timing-side shaft and the flywheels are ready for the main assembly. Whilst the figure of 0·005 in. is fairly easy to

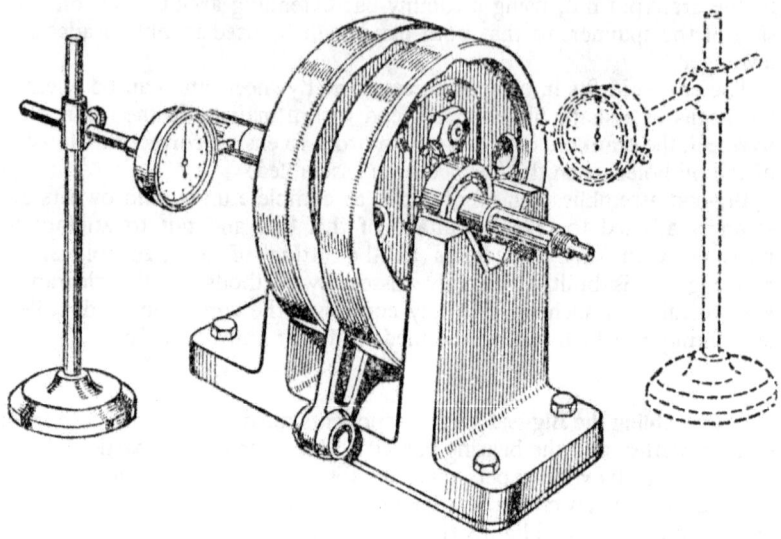

FIG. 49. USING A DIAL INDICATOR TO CHECK FLYWHEEL ALIGNMENT

obtain, patience and no small amount of skill are required to bring the alignment to within 0·002 in. as so much depends upon striking the wheels in the right place. Accurate mainshaft alignment will not only assist assembly, but also avoid bearing and other troubles later on.

Crankcase Assembly. On the timing side of the crankcase, examine the housing carrying the mainshaft bearing in which, on later models, a $\frac{1}{32}$ in. hole was drilled. This should be added to the earlier models. Drill the hole through the top of the housing at an angle of 45 degrees starting $\frac{1}{16}$ in. from the crankcase wall, and stopping as soon as the drill breaks through into the annular groove on the outside of the bearing—a distance of about $\frac{3}{16}$ in.

Thoroughly clean the crankcase halves (especially after reaming any new bushes), particularly their joint faces. At all stages of assembly, every bearing surface must be well lubricated with engine oil, because for a short time after reassembly, this will be the only lubricant available until the oil begins to circulate from the pump.

Place the oil-flinger washer onto the drive-side mainshaft (this will mean

DISMANTLING AND REASSEMBLY OF THE ENGINE

there is one on each side of the ballrace), pass the shaft through the bearing and gently tap the drive-side half of the crankcase into position over the mainshaft, until the ballrace is firmly against the flywheel. Add a thin coat of jointing compound to the joint faces of the crankcase halves, and replace the timing side, locking them together by means of their studs. Before proceeding further, put the assembly into a vice as when dismantling, and check that the flywheels rotate freely. Do not allow the connecting-rod to damage the crankcase mouth when carrying out this test. If the shafts are not rotating freely, it may be that they are not properly aligned, or that the crankcase plain bearing is not line-reamed accurately. In either case, the crankcase will have to be dismantled again for careful checking and the faults remedied.

Replace the oil pump and slide the driving spindle into position, retaining it with its pin which must have the tongue engaged in the spindle groove. If a washer was fitted in front of the pin, be sure to replace it, but if not, a washer can be added to make certain that the spindle and tongue engage. In this case, take care that the tongue does not fit too tightly when the timing cover is replaced. Refit the key to the timing-slide mainshaft and add the pinion, tapping it home with a tubular drift and then locking with the nut and tab washer.

Examine the cam surfaces and those of the cam followers. If badly worn, or if rapid wear has developed on previous occasions, modified followers can be obtained for the O.H.V. model, with bearing pads of a specially hard material, which overcome the problem and provide a greatly improved life. Replace the cam followers with their spacer sleeve and do not omit the circlip. As the camshaft is returned to its normal position, rotate its driving gear so that the timing mark opposite a gap between two teeth, registers with a tooth on the mainshaft pinion, which is similarly marked. This part of the assembly and that of the timing cover is described under "Valve Timing," page 23. Add the advance-and-retard mechanism and make sure that the peg on the spindle engages in the groove in the camshaft before tightening the central nut. At this point it will be as well to reassemble the piston, rings, and gudgeon-pin in readiness for ignition timing, for which purpose the contact-breaker should next be remounted. The instructions given on page 19 for ignition timing can be followed, except that it will be simplified by replacing the cylinder barrel (*see* page 75) because the position of the piston can then be determined precisely. Note that the ignition timing is a dimension given for the piston distance from the top of its stroke and not from the top of the barrel.

Little remains to be done on the driving side of the engine except to add the drilled sleeve, which is so designed that it is immaterial on which spline it is positioned. It must be fitted with the holes nearest to the flywheel. The engine is now ready for returning to the frame, and when in position, do not forget to tighten the nuts on the gearbox yoke plates which were slackened to facilitate removal of the engine. Feed the contact-breaker lead through the gearbox shield, which can then be bolted in position and the lead connected to the contact-breaker. Replace the inner half of the primary chaincase, and reassemble the engine-shaft sprocket, alternator housing, and the alternator. The mainshaft nut must be tightened securely, as it takes up all the crankshaft end-float, and retained with its locking washer.

The clutch can now be remounted on the gearbox mainshaft (*see* assembly details on page 48), and the actuation checked. Replace the primary chain, the outer half of the chaincase, footrest, etc., and replenish the case with engine oil to the level plug.

Assembling the remainder of the engine is as detailed in the chapter on decarbonizing (page 66). Connect the oil pipes to the crankcase, making sure that they go to the correct unions, one of which is marked "return" for the pipe carrying oil back to the tank. Refill the latter to its correct level with the recommended lubricant as given on page 4.

250 STAR ENGINE

As already explained, it is preferable to carry out as much dismantling as possible while the engine is still in the frame.

First, then, dismantle the engine down to the level of the crankcase face as described in the section "Decarbonizing the Engine," page 66, which also gives details on removal of the petrol tank and other items. Next, the clutch can be taken off, and this task includes the dismantling of the primary chain and alternator unit, details being given under "Removal and Replacement of the Clutch" (*see* page 46). Dismantling the gearbox is described in the section "Clutch and Gearbox" (*see* page 40).

Drain the oil tank and disconnect the pipe lines to the crankcase at their common union below the case. It will also be necessary to take off the rear chainguard, and uncouple the rear chain if it has not already been removed. Disconnect the leads from the alternator at their snap connectors behind the chaincase and note carefully the positions and colours of the various cables for reassembly purposes.

The crankcase is held in the frame at three points. To enable the rear fixing stud to be readily removed, the front of the engine must be raised slightly. Disengage from the frame brackets and lift the engine out from the near side. At this stage, the timing gears will be exposed, as the inner timing cover will have been taken off in order to dismantle the gearbox. Raise the tappets to their highest position so as to clear the cams, and pull out the camshaft and its gearwheel, afterwards withdrawing the tappets downwards into the timing chest. Note that the tappet lubricating holes face the rear. When the timing cover was removed, the distributor clip was automatically released (this is visible in Fig. 17), so that the distributor itself can now be drawn out. Note that the clip has a plain hole in one side and a threaded one in the opposite side; it must be replaced with the plain hole towards the outside of the engine. The distributor and clip were replaced for the 1965 season by a contact-breaker unit mounted on the crankcase, the place of the distributor being taken by a screwed plug. This must be taken out before the oil-pump spindle (which replaces the distributor drive shaft) can be driven upwards.

Next take off the sump cover and filter below the crankcase, and release the oil pump, for which there is just sufficient space to take it out through the timing case. The pump is retained by the three screws (*see* Fig. 50), the other screws holding the pump assembly together. If the efficiency of the pump is in doubt it is advisable not to dismantle it but to obtain a new unit. Removal of the pump leaves the way clear for the insertion of a ⅜ in. soft drift to the face of the distributor drive shaft (or oil-pump spindle after 1964), which must be driven upwards until it is clear of the worm wheel on the engine mainshaft. It is important to note that

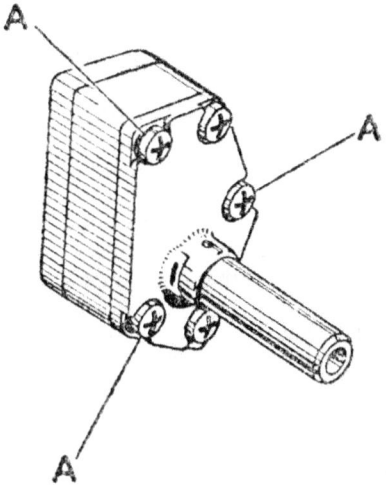

FIG. 50. ON 250 STAR MODELS (UP TO 1966) THE OIL PUMP IS RETAINED BY THREE SCREWS
The remaining two screws hold the pump assembly together.

on engines numbered from 9009, the distributor shaft bush is locked in position by a grub-screw which must be removed before the bush can be moved.

Unscrew the mainshaft nut after straightening its tag washer and take the pinion off the shaft. In all probability this will require the use of an extractor, which can be obtained from a B.S.A. dealer under Part No. 61-3681, together with extractor jaws Part No. 61-3588. Removal of the worm wheel follows next, again using the same extractor but with jaws Part No. 61-3585. Note carefully which way the worm wheel is fitted. Seven bolts or studs hold the crankcase halves together, the bolts being at the front of the case, whilst the stud nuts are found at the cylinder base and in the primary chaincase. The two halves register with each other, and if jointing compound has been used on the mating faces, a few blows with a soft mallet may be required to free them.

The timing side of the case is fitted with a plain bearing for the crankshaft, so that this side is the first to be removed, leaving the flywheel and mainshaft assembly in the drive-side half of the case. Some assistance may be required in parting the drive-side mainshaft from the case. Hold the latter above the bench with the drive-side mainshaft uppermost, so that the assistant can strike the end of the mainshaft with a lead hammer, driving it through the bearing to the inside of the case. The flywheels may be released suddenly, and they should be poised at a minimum distance above the bench throughout this operation. The collar between the ballrace and the sprocket is fitted with the chamfered edge outwards, and it must be replaced in this position.

Adjacent to the flywheel on the timing-side mainshaft, a sleeve is pressed on to the shaft, and if this is to be removed, another extractor is necessary under B.S.A. Part No. 61–3593. To remove the mainshaft ballrace, first heat the case by immersing in hot water and apply a suitable drift from the outside of the case. While this is still warm, refit the new bearing, using a tubular punch on the outer ring of the bearing. When the old bearing has been taken out the oil-seal can be tapped out of position, and a replacement seal must be fitted with its lip towards the inside of the engine. Plain bearings can also be removed much easier after heating the cases or covers, and new ones must be carefully reamed to size after fitting.

Should it be decided that the big-end requires replacement, the whole assembly should be obtained as a unit. (*See also* (page 81) *Dismantling and Reassembly of the big-end.*)

Alternatively, if the big-end is in good order, there is no necessity to dismantle the flywheels but, with these out of the crankcase, it is a suitable opportunity to attend to the sludge trap situated in the rim of the timing-side flywheel. This is clearly shown at *F* (*see* Fig. 2). Take out the screw and turn the flywheels until the aperture is downwards, so that as the sludge is loosened, there is no likelihood of particles falling into the oilways. The trap acts as a final filter for the oil flowing to the big-end. If there has not been any sign of oil transference from the tank to the crankcase, it indicates that the ball valve *A* (*see* Fig. 2) is in good order and should not be disturbed, as the metal round the grub-screw has been burred over as a security means. At the same time, dismantle and clean the by-pass valve *D*, Fig. 2.

Notes on Engine Reassembly. Assuming that the mainshaft ball bearing and oil-seal have been renewed if required, the crankcase and flywheels are now ready for assembly. The flywheels and mainshaft should be supported in a vertical position with the drive-side shaft at the top and the timing-side shaft just clear of the bench. Now feed the drive-side half of the crankcase into position on the shaft and tap down until it is certain that the face of the flywheel is firmly against the ball bearing. Replace the spacing collar which fits against the outer face of the bearing, remembering to have the chamfered edge outwards.

Smear a little jointing compound on the joint faces of the crankcase halves, slide the timing-side half into position, and tighten the nuts or bolts evenly a little at a time in order to prevent distortion of the case. Examine the mainshaft worm gear and its mating gear on the distributor drive shaft for signs of excessive wear which, if present, may cause variations in the ignition timing (on models produced in 1965-6, this does not affect the ignition timing). Modified gears were introduced at engine No. 11715 and as they are not interchangeable with the previous type, a pair of the new gears must be obtained for the earlier models if necessary. Fit the mainshaft key and drive both worm gear and timing pinion fully home. Note that in both cases they must be fitted the correct way round, i.e. the worm gear has its extension outwards and that of the timing pinion inwards. Tighten the mainshaft nut securely and lock with its tab washer. Set the crankpin at its uppermost position.

The distributor drive shaft and its bush can next be replaced from the top, the bush being inserted with its oil groove downwards, and the slot in the end of the shaft parallel with the crankshaft. Tap the bush gently down to the bottom of the housing bore, noting that the shaft turns to a new position as the gears engage. For models made in 1965-6, when the oil-pump spindle superseded the distributor drive shaft, replace the spindle in the shaft aperture and engage the teeth with those on the mainshaft worm. Place the spindle bush into position from the top of the aperture and gently tap downwards until the groove in the bush is level with the screw hole in the housing. Add the grub screw and re-fit the plug at the top of the aperture.

Make certain that the gear is free to rotate easily with a minimum of up-and-down play, and that the circular groove in the bush is level with the screw hole. Check this by temporary insertion of the screw and, if satisfactory, lock in position by means of the small grub screw (later models only).

Bolt the oil pump in position, its driving tongue registering with the slot in the distributor shaft, and here it should be noted that really clean joint faces are necessary, together with the use of a new gasket coated very lightly with jointing compound. Replace the filter cover and gaskets, once again using compound to ensure an oiltight joint. Rotate the flywheels again until the crankpin is at the top of its stroke, and insert the tappets into their guide holes. Retain these in position and replace the camshaft complete with its gear, so that the timing mark on the teeth coincides with a corresponding mark on the engine shaft pinion (*see* Fig. 17).

The distributor clip is next to be replaced in its recess in the crankcase (*see* Fig. 17), and then slide the distributor into position through the clip, making sure that its driving tongue engages with the slot in the driving shaft. Although the distributor is now in position, the ignition timing cannot be set because its retaining clip is fixed by one of the outer timing cover screws (E, Fig. 17), and this cover is one of the last items to be fitted on this side of the engine. It involves reassembly of the gearbox, as detailed in the chapter "Clutch and Gearbox" (*see* page 41), and subsequent reassembly of the remainder of the timing side of the crankcase, as given under "Valve Timing" (*see* page 23). At this point it will be as well to return the crankcase to the frame, and complete the assembly of the engine in position. It will simplify the setting of the ignition timing if it is carried out following replacement of the piston and cylinder barrel, when the piston position can be determined accurately. This applies equally to the distributor type of contact-breaker unit used prior to 1965 and to the crankcase contact-breaker used thereafter. This operation is described under "Ignition Timing" (*see* page 19), and a reminder must be given here that when the piston is at the top of its stroke, it is not necessarily at the top of the barrel. The remainder of the engine assembly is completed from the instructions given for "Decarbonizing the Engine" (*see* page 66). Assembly of the clutch, primary chain and alternator are described in the chapter "Clutch and Gearbox."

250 STAR (1967), BARRACUDA AND STARFIRE ENGINES

The instructions given in the previous chapter for removal of the 250 Star engine from its frame, also apply to these engines, while the procedures for prior dismantling of the top half, removal of the clutch and primary drive, removal of timing covers and the gear cluster, are as given in the earlier chapters.

Because of appreciable 1967 engine modifications subsequent dismantling is different in some respects from engines built before that year, but these notes should still be studied in conjunction with those for the 250 Star.

When the above stages are completed and the engine is on the bench, withdraw the camshaft and pinion which are keyed together (note the timing marks for re-assembly purposes). This allows the tappets to fall clear and be removed. Next unscrew the crankshaft nut, having first straightened its tab-washer. Here, it may be found necessary to prevent rotation of the shaft by inserting a bar through the connecting-rod small-end. Draw off the crankshaft pinion, followed by the oil pump worm and thrust washer. The B.S.A. extractor (No. 61-3773) should be applied for this purpose, using the appropriate legs for each component. Next take off the oil pump. It is not advisable to dismantle this; if it is suspected of being faulty, a new unit should be obtained from a B.S.A. dealer. Remove the sump filter, oil pipe union and any keys remaining in the shafts.

As on the 250 Star, seven bolts or studs unite the crankcase halves. Ball journals are used on both sides of the flywheels and, to part the crankcase, the services of an assistant will be required. Hold the complete case with crankshaft vertical (gearside uppermost) and give the shaft a sharp blow with a lead hammer, enabling the drive side half, complete with crankshaft, to be drawn free. Turn this case over, and drive out the crankshaft in a similar manner. Do not use wedges of any description between the crankcase joint faces. Note that there is a shim fitted to the gear side of the crankshaft to provide limited end-float.

The crankshaft ball journals can be driven out after heating the case in hot water and, while still warm, fit the new bearings and oil seal (lip to the *inside* of the engine). The flywheel sludge trap F, ball valve A, and by-pass valve D (Fig. 2), can receive attention as described for the 250 Star (*see* page 86).

The 250 Star (1967) was fitted with a roller bearing big-end and reference should be made to the earlier 250 Star for any attention that may be required.

On the Barracuda and Starfire engines, thin-wall shell bearings are used for the big-end and these are released when the bearing cap is removed. Mark the cap and connecting-rod to ensure reassembly the same way round and note the position of the small oil hole in the rod. A worn or scored crankpin will require the crankshaft assembly to be returned to a B.S.A. dealer for re-grinding and the fitting of suitable shell bearings. It is most important that the bearing surfaces are not scraped in any way, nor the connecting rod and cap faces filed.

Reassembly of the connecting-rod requires scrupulous cleanliness and a liberal coating of engine oil should be applied to the bearing surfaces. Make sure the rod and cap are correctly fitted together and that the oil hole is facing in the same direction as when removed. Use new self-locking nuts which must be tightened with a torque of 25–27 lb. ft. Check that all oilways are clear by applying a pressure oil-can to the end of the crankshaft and injecting oil until it excludes at the big-end.

Notes on Engine Reassembly. The crankcase halves can be reassembled as explained for the 250 Star, but for the Barracuda and Starfire engines, the crankshaft end-float should be limited to 0·002–0·006 in. If necessary, separate the crankcase halves again and modify the shim thickness between crankshaft and timing-side bearing, until this figure is obtained.

Tighten the crankcase bolts and studs as evenly as possible to avoid distortion of the joint faces. Check that the crankshaft rotates freely and if found satisfactory, fit the sprocket collar (chamfer *outward*) to the drive side and the worm thrust washer (also chamfer *outward*) to the gear side of the crankshaft. Sprocket collars are obtainable in various widths to ensure precise chain alignment.

Replace the oil pump, using a *new* gasket lightly smeared with jointing compound, and tighten the two fixing nuts with a torque of 7 lb. ft. Fit the pump worm on to the crankshaft together with its driving key and then add the timing pinion and locking nut. Tighten firmly and secure with the tab-washer. Replace the crankcase filter and gasket, again using a little jointing compound.

Re-position the tappets. On the Barracuda and Starfire engines it is most important that the *thinner* edge of each tappet foot is *towards the front* of the engine. The 250 Star tappets must be replaced with the stem oil holes towards the *rear* of the engine. Now add the large timing pinion, making sure that the timing marks coincide as shown in Fig. 17, and replace the oil pipe union. Do not forget their "O" ring oil seals, otherwise there will be serious air or oil leaks.

At this point, reference should be made to other sections in this maintenance handbook for the remainder of the assembly. The gear cluster, inner and outer timing covers with their associated parts are dealt with in Chapter III. Instructions for reassembling of the clutch, primary chain, alternator, etc. are included.

Return the crankcase to the frame, fit the piston and cylinder barrel, and re-set the ignition timing before replacing the cylinder head (*see* "Ignition timing, page 19). Further engine assembly instructions are as given under Decarbonizing the Engine (*see* page 66).

Important notes for 1969–70 Starfire models
1. For the commencement of the 1969 season, B.S.A. largely adopted the unified thread system, replacing many of the B.S.F., B.S.W., etc, threads with the new form.

Not all components were changed over, because suitable threads were not always available in the unified system (especially the larger diameters with fine threads), but the majority of bolts, studs, etc., were so changed.

When replacements for these items are required, check that their threads correspond, particularly in the case of captive nuts and similar items.

2. Provision is made for driving a tachometer (or revolution counter) from the crankcase, the driving shaft aperture being covered by a small sealing plate, as standard specification.

A complete kit of parts for fitting a tachometer can be obtained from the B.S.A. Spares Dept., under part No 00-5195.

6 Steering and Suspension

THE steering head bearing is perhaps one of the most important on a motor-cycle and yet it is one which all too often is neglected. Test the head occasionally for play by supporting the crankcase on a box, so that the front wheel is clear of the ground. Stand astride the wheel, grasp the fork legs and attempt to push them backwards and forwards. If any play is detected, the head bearings must be adjusted. If they have been allowed to become too slack, and have run in this condition for some time, the balls will in all probability have dented their races, making accurate adjustment impossible. If these indentations can be felt when turning the handlebars, it will be necessary to dismantle the head and replace the cups and cones. On the other hand, if the adjustment is made too close, the steering will be stiff and uncomfortable, and may even be dangerous. When the adjustment is completed, hold the handlebars lightly and move them round slowly, when the steering should be free and rotate smoothly. This latter point is most important.

Adjustment of the Head Bearings. C10L, C11G AND C12 MODELS. On all models, except the C10L, the steering-stem cap nut B (Fig. 51) is directly accessible, but on the C10L the nut is covered by a small shield which clamps the handlebars, and this must first be removed by unscrewing the four nuts beneath it. Unscrew the cap, slacken clip bolt C, and *release the clip bolts locking the fork legs into the lower steering yoke.* This is to allow the yoke to take up a new position on the legs. Tighten sleeve D until the slackness is only just eliminated, retighten the three clip bolts, and replace cap nut B.

250 STAR, BARRACUDA AND STARFIRE MODELS. Adjustment is similar to that just described except that sleeve D is not provided, and play in the head is taken up by movement of cap nut B directly.

Replacement of the Head Bearings. C11G AND C12 MODELS. Place a support beneath the crankcase so that the front wheel is clear of the ground. It is not essential during this operation to remove the wheel, but if this is done it will reduce the weight to be handled and is therefore preferable. Disconnect the front brake and clutch cables at the handlebar levers and also release the headlamp dip-switch. Next, remove the lighting switch from the lamp and draw the switch and harness through the rubber grommet at the back of the lamp. The switch knob is retained by a small grub screw and when the knob is removed the fixing nut is exposed, and this must be unscrewed to release the switch body. The speedometer cable must be uncoupled just below the instrument, together with its lighting bulb.

Referring now to Fig. 51, unscrew the cap nut B and the fork leg nuts A. Slacken the clip bolt C, and unscrew the adjuster sleeve D two or three turns only. At this point precautions should be taken to support the fork leg assembly because, at the next operation, the steering column will be released. The fork legs are retained in the top yoke by a taper engagement

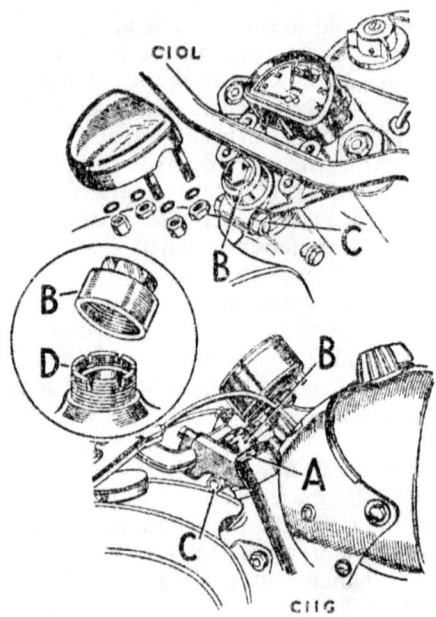

FIG. 51. ADJUSTMENT TO THE STEERING HEAD ON MODELS C10L, C11G AND C12

On the 250 Star, Barracuda, and Starfire the sleeve D is omitted, otherwise the systems are similar.

and a sharp blow on the underside of the yoke will free the legs. Still supporting the legs unscrew the sleeve D fully so that the top yoke, together with the handlebars, the upper cone, and its dust shield can be lifted off. Lower the fork assembly, comprising forks, lamp, steering column, etc., until the column can be drawn from below the head. All the balls from the top and bottom bearings will have been released, but no harm has been done, because they must not be used again. New $\frac{3}{16}$ in. balls must be fitted on reassembly and there are 24 of these in each of the bearings.

The cups remaining in the steering head can be taken out with the aid of a simple extractor, which is screwed firmly into the cup and then driven out from the opposite end of the head, carrying the cup with it. The extractor comprises a short length of 1⅜ in. bar threaded 24 t.p.i. B.S.C.

The cone at the lower end of the steering stem may be a little more difficult to remove and requires a wedge-shaped drift driven between the cone and the yoke, being applied at evenly spaced intervals. The new cone must be driven firmly on to its seat by means of a piece of tubing of such a bore, that it just fits over the steering column, and sits on the top face of the cone.

New cups must be driven squarely into the steering head using a flat plate across the cups. It is essential that these (and the cone) are pressed well home, otherwise they will settle down after assembly, and slacken off the adjustment.

When replacing the column, coat the ball tracks liberally with grease to retain the balls in position. Deal similarly with the upper bearing, then add the dust shield, top yoke, and adjuster sleeve. Screw up the fork leg nuts A (*see* Fig. 51) firmly. Adjust the bearings so that the column turns freely but without play (*see* page 91), when the clip bolt (C) can be tightened and the remainder of the assembly completed.

C10L MODEL ONLY. Construction of the forks on this model is slightly different from that for the C12 model, due to the fact that they are not hydraulically damped. Dismantling instructions in general follow those already given, except that the fork nuts A (Fig. 51), require their centre caps to be prised out of position in order to expose the spring locking nut. This must be removed before the main nut can be unscrewed.

250 STAR. With few exceptions the instructions given for the C12 also apply to this model. As the headlamp is mounted in a nacelle, the lighting cables will have to be disconnected at their snap connectors behind the reflector. Also within the nacelle, detach the wires to the ammeter and then unscrew the lighting switch centre screw and take off the knob, which will expose the nut locking the switch into the nacelle. Release this nut, and the switch can then be pushed into the nacelle and drawn out from the back. Note carefully the colours and positions of all the disconnected cables, so as to avoid trouble on reassembly.

On later models and also for separate headlamps, the switch connexions are by plug and socket which are easily separated. It will also be necessary to disconnect the speedometer drive.

Removal of the cups from the steering head does not require an extractor and they can be driven out from the opposite end with a suitable punch. Referring to Fig. 51, the adjuster sleeve D is not used on these models.

BARRACUDA AND STARFIRE MODELS. Most of the instructions given for the C11G and C12 machines apply also to these models, but it will be advisable to uncouple the headlamp to allow extra slackness in the wiring, and also to remove the speedometer and zener-diode, complete with finned carrier. Extract the handlebar fixing bolts and lay the bars on the tank. Slacken the clip bolts which lock the fork legs into the lower steering yoke, followed by the top yoke pinch-bolt C (Fig. 51) and take off the adjuster nut B. Unscrew and raise the cap nuts A until the lock-nut on the rod below can be unscrewed and the nut removed.

Now support the fork leg assembly and apply a sharp blow to the underside of the top yoke to free it from the fork tubes. This will release the steering stem which can be withdrawn from the steering head. Forty $\frac{1}{4}$ in. diameter balls will also be released. The cones should be removed in the manner previously described for the C11G and C12 models and the cups by using B.S.A. Service Tool No. 61-3063.

Replacement of the cups and cones should be done as described for the earlier models, except that it is preferable for the cups to be driven into position with the aid of a steel bar slightly smaller in diameter than the outside of each cup. The ball tracks must *not* be touched.

Before replacing the steering stem, coat the ball tracks liberally with grease to retain the new balls in position. Deal similarly with the upper bearing and then re-fit the stem into position in the head. Replace the top cone, dust cover and top yoke. Retain in position with the adjuster nut B (Fig. 51), leaving the hands free for the remainder of the reassembly.

Front Fork Hydraulic Damping. There is no provision for hydraulic damping of the fork springs of the 1954–5 C10L model, but on all others, provided that the oil level is maintained, the damping is automatic and no adjustment is necessary or provided. Normally, all that is required is draining and re-filling both fork legs with fresh S.A.E. 20 oil at intervals of 10,000 miles (*see* page 4).

A small drain screw is provided at the bottom of each fork leg. Remove the fork leg top nut A (*see* Fig. 51) which, in addition to holding the leg in position also acts as a filler cap, and then drain out the old oil. To remove the last traces of oil, apply the front brake and depress the forks a few times. Replace the drain plug and add oil as follows—to the C10L (1956), C11G and C12 machines—$\frac{1}{4}$ pint; to the 250 Star machine—$\frac{1}{6}$ pint; to the 250 Star Trials and Scrambles Model—$\frac{1}{8}$ pint; to the Barracuda and Starfire—$\frac{1}{8}$ pint. Replace the top nut securely as if this be allowed to become loose, the steering may be adversely affected.

Hydraulic Rear Suspension Units. The spring strengths are determined by the manufacturers to give a good all-round performance, but for use under exceptional conditions, it may be that stronger springs would give a more comfortable ride. Early C12 machines were fitted with springs of moderate strength, but after frame No. 7477 the strength was increased by about 25 per cent, and if the suspension on the early machines is considered to be too "soft," the latest springs (Part No. 29–4560) should be fitted. In both cases, the springs are very strong and if the original ones are to be removed the job must be done carefully to avoid damage to the fingers. The springs are retained by two circlips, and must be compressed a short distance before the circlips can be taken out. Because of the spring strength, this is not an easy matter without a special tool, and one

STEERING AND SUSPENSION

of these can be obtained from a B.S.A. dealer under Part No. 61-5064 for the C12 models.

The same tool is suitable for the 250 Star model. Also, on this model, stronger springs were introduced from engine No. 31287.

Service tool No. 61-3503 is required for dismantling the rear suspension units on the Barracuda and Starfire models.

Rear Suspension (Plunger Type). When overhaul is considered necessary or if, on a rare occasion, a broken spring is to be replaced, the suspension unit can be withdrawn as a whole.

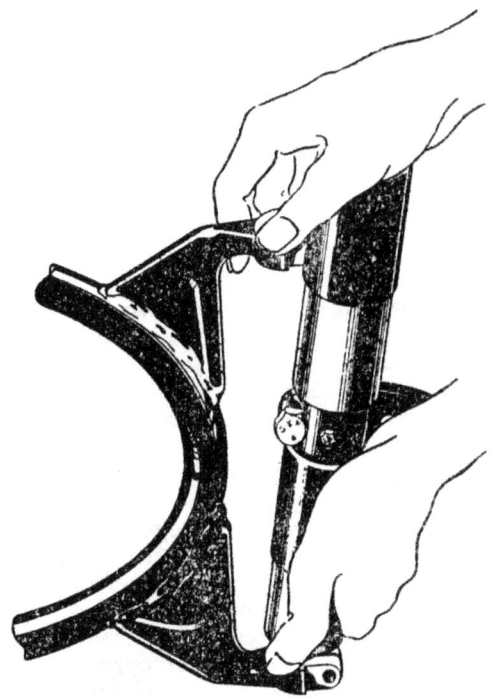

FIG. 52. FITTING THE PLUNGER REAR SUSPENSION UNITS

First remove the rear wheel as explained on page 37. Then disconnect the mudguard stays and take out the clip bolts A and B (*see* Fig. 23) in the frame lugs above and below the suspension units. This leaves the central column free, and it can be driven out with a soft punch.

It is now possible to remove the suspension unit complete, by slightly compressing the upper and lower spring covers, and withdrawing out of the frame.

Check the sliding tube bushes for wear, and if they require renewal, both tube and bushes should be replaced. The sliding tube is clamped in the fork end lug, and removal of the bolt C (*see* Fig. 23) allows the tube to be taken out. This will be made easier if a screwdriver is inserted into the slot, so that the lug can be opened a little to free the tube.

When the new tube is fitted, it is most important to ensure that the clip bolt on the offside is replaced in its correct position, as its head secures the brake cover plate, and that the grease nipple in the fork-end lines up with the hole in the sliding tube.

Reassemble the complete suspension units, and place the lower spring cover on to the frame lug (*see* Fig. 52). Compress the upper spring shroud and slide the whole assembly into position between the lugs. Line up the slots on the central columns with the pinch bolts and insert the column from the top. Lock the clip bolt firmly and replace the mudguards and wheel.

The "Swinging Arm" Suspension. Earlier models utilized rubber-bonded bushes at the fulcrum, whilst on the later ones (the C15 Star group) the "swinging arm" oscillates on phosphor-bronze bearings, and it is unlikely that any of these bearings will need replacement for a considerable time.

C12 MODELS. First place a support beneath the machine so that the rear wheel is clear of the ground, and remove the wheel in accordance with the instructions on page 37. Next, take off the chainguard and then the two suspension units, so that the "swinging arm" is completely free.

Release the fulcrum spindle nut on the offside (a self-locking nut which must be used at this point), and the spindle anchorage at the opposite end. Drive the spindle out of position, which will require a rod slightly smaller in diameter than the spindle. Raise the "swinging arm" until it is clear of the yoke plates, turn it on one side, and withdraw from the rear.

The rubber-bonded bushes are difficult to remove, but perhaps the easiest way is to strike the centre tube sharply, so that the long spacer sleeve between the bushes can fall out of position. This will allow a rod of suitable size to be inserted through one of the bushes to drive out the one on the opposite side. The spacer sleeve will then fall out and the remaining bush can be driven out. The success of this operation depends upon the ease with which the spacer sleeve is displaced and if this should prove impossible, the alternative is to burn away the rubber from one of the bushes. This is best carried out with the aid of thin metal strips or rods which have been heated.

Replace the new offside bush first and press into position until its largest diameter is just level with the outer end face of its housing. Add the central spacer sleeve and temporarily replace the fulcrum pin, so that when the second bush is fitted, all three components will be in line. Drive the bush into its housing until the spacer is gripped between the two bushes and then remove the fulcrum pin.

Return the fork to the frame and reinsert the fulcrum pin, but do not

STEERING AND SUSPENSION 97

tighten the nut at this stage. Complete the reassembly of all other items and then attend to the position of the "swinging arm" before tightening the spindle nut. Replace the machine on its wheels and load the rear wheel until the suspension is at the centre of its travel. Now tighten the fulcrum spindle nut securely. This is an essential part of the assembly procedure and ensures that the bushes are clamped in correct relationship to the "swinging arm." The loading of the machine will, in all probability, require the services of an assistant, especially while the nut is being tightened.

250 STAR. The "swinging arm" pivots should be regularly lubricated, as under bad weather conditions they are subjected to contact with mud and water, flung up by the rear wheel. Rapid wear of these bearings is usually

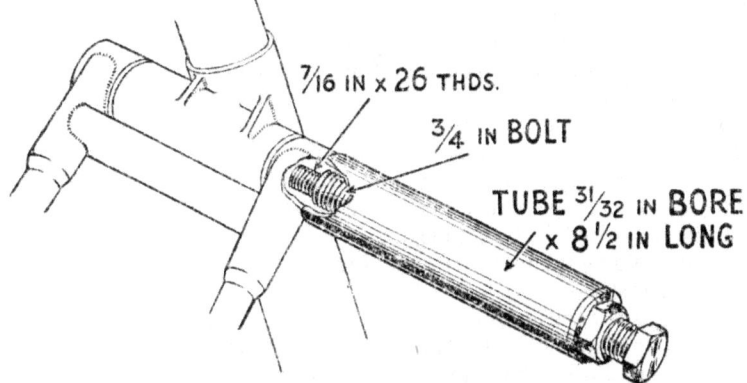

FIG. 53. "SWINGING ARM" SPINDLE EXTRACTOR (250 STAR)

a sign of neglect. To replace the bushes involves almost complete dismantling of the rear part of the frame, together with the fabrication of a withdrawal tool for the spindle.

First take out the rear wheel as described on page 37, followed by the chain guard. Next, take off the dualseat (fixed at the upper suspension unit anchorages) and then unbolt the coil, horn, and rectifier from the sub-frame cross member. Uncouple the tail light at its snap connector near the tool box, and remove the mudguard which is attached to the loop of the sub-frame and to the main frame. Remove the two suspension units and this will allow the sub-frame to be taken off (a single bolt connexion near the petrol tank, and a bolt at each end of the "swinging arm" spindle). Early models were lubricated via a grease nipple in the spindle mounting lug and this should be taken out in case it should restrict withdrawal of the spindle.

The spindle will be found to be extremely tight in the frame lug, and to remove it will necessitate an extractor similar to that shown in Fig. 53, which can be constructed from odds and ends by most handymen. Take out the "swinging arm" and, supporting each pivot in turn, drive out the bushes with the aid of a steel rod of suitable size. When new bushes are fitted, they must be inserted squarely into their housing with their joints towards the engine, and care must be taken not to damage their faces. Once they have been pressed in, the bushes should be line-reamed to restore the correct bore size, and the spindle used as a test piece. It must rotate freely and without play.

Thoroughly grease the moving parts, replace the "swinging arm" in position, and push the spindle through one of the bushes. Add the thrust washers and feed the bolt (previously used for extraction purposes) through the opposite bush, screwing into the spindle end. Tighten the nut and draw the spindle into its normal position, until it is flush with the faces of the "swinging arm." This is essential so that the sub-frame members will not bind against the "swinging arm" and as soon as it has been refitted, check that the "swinging arm" moves freely. Reassembly does not call for special comment except that this may be considered to be a suitable opportunity for cleaning and lubricating the rear chain (page 9), checking the alignment of the wheels (page 33), and examining the rear brake.

BARRACUDA AND STARFIRE MODELS. The swinging-arm pivots on rubber-bonded bushes, and the removal of the arm and extraction of the bushes are as described previously for model C12. Naturally it will be necessary to remove the complete rear wheel assembly (not just the wheel alone) and also the brake pedal. Uncouple the stop-light switch connexions, release the bolts holding the pillion footrest bracket to the frame and remove the brake-pedal stop.

Now unscrew the large nut which holds the off-side end of the spindle and drive the latter out. It is important to note that this nut must not be tightened until *after* the damper units have been replaced, and also that it is not necessary to pre-load the dampers before tightening the nut. Tap the near side of the swinging arm downwards and the off side upwards to release the arm from the frame.

On Barracuda and Starfire models the spacer sleeve has been discontinued, the centre sleeve on each bush being lengthened accordingly; when new sleeves are fitted they must project by equal amounts at each side of the pivot.

Removing the Fork Leg Bushes. Before attempting to remove the fork legs all other fittings must be taken off. First place a support beneath the crankcase so that the front wheel is clear of the ground and then remove the wheel as detailed on page 37, followed by the mudguard and stays. On all models except the 1954–5 C10L, the hydraulic fluid must be drained off as described on page 94.

C10L 1954–5. Access to the sleeve bearings on these machines can be gained without the use of an extractor. Free the top end of the telescopic gaiter from the oil-seal holder and slide it down the lower tube, so uncovering the holder which can be unscrewed after releasing its locking clip. At the upper end of the fork leg, prise out the small cap in the centre of the nut, to expose the smaller spring securing nut, and when this has been unscrewed, the fork sliding tube, complete with spring and rubber damping

STEERING AND SUSPENSION 99

tube, can be withdrawn from the lower end of the fixed tube. To remove the spring, it can be unwound from its "scroll" if the lower leg is held in a vice (with suitable clamps to suit the tube to prevent injury) and a small punch is used to tap the end of the spring. This operation is also necessary if the rubber tube is to be taken out. Unscrew the grease nipple from the fixed tube and draw out the lower bush. This will leave a long spacer sleeve and the top bush still in position, both of which can be pulled out with the aid of a spoke or something similar.

It is not normally necessary to dismount the fixed tube but this can be done if required by releasing the clip bolt on the lower steering stem yoke, followed by the large nut on the top yoke. If the latter is unscrewed two or three turns and then given a sharp blow with a mallet, it will release the tube from its taper seating, when the nut can be unscrewed and the tube drawn downwards through the lower yoke. The slots in this yoke should be opened slightly with a screwdriver to allow the tube to slide freely through the bush.

Examine the bushes and sliding tube for wear, replacing as required and fit a new oil-seal. If the gaiter shows signs of splitting, this, too, must be renewed, as it forms the sole protection for the exposed portion of the sliding tube.

When reassembling, liberally coat the working parts with grease and note that the spacer sleeve is fitted so that its slot is in line with the grease nipple. Tighten the oil-seal holder firmly, as this has the added purpose of clamping the bushes in the fixed tube, and also make sure that the spring securing nut is quite tight before covering it with the cap.

1956 C10L, C11G, C12. On all these models, the fork construction is such that dismantling cannot be undertaken without the aid of extractors, of which several are required and it is of little use attempting the job without them. They can be obtained through any B.S.A. dealer, but as the cost is likely to be heavy it may be as well to have the work carried out by the dealer. For those who wish to do the dismantling for themselves a study of the following notes should simplify the procedure.

Slacken the clip bolt which clamps the fork shaft to the lower steering stem yoke, and unscrew the cap nut at the top of the fork shaft (*see* Fig. 51). This nut pulls the shaft into a taper seating in the top yoke, and to release it insert a screwed plug into the thread exposed by removal of the cap nut. A sharp blow on the end of the plug will release the fork shaft, which can then be drawn through the lower yoke. A suitable screwed plug is incorporated in service tool Part No. 61-3350, the use of which will be essential when the time comes to replace the shaft, because of the powerful spring which has to be compressed.

Hold the fork assembly in a vice with suitable clams in the jaws and, after lifting out the spring, slide the special tool Part No. 61-3005 over the shaft and down the tubular sleeve, to engage with the slots in the spring seating (*see* Fig. 54 indicated at D). The sleeve, seating, and oil-seal can be unscrewed together. The upper part of the fork shaft is tapered and once the sleeve is clear of its threads, it must not be moved too far along the shaft, otherwise the oil-seal may be expanded excessively and ruined. The sleeve can be removed from the other end of the shaft at a later stage.

A round-wire circlip will now be exposed and this must be prised out of position. Next, pull out the fork shaft complete with oil-seal and sleeve circlip, and the two bushes. The top bush may be a little tight in the sliding tube and the shaft may require a sharp jerk to draw it out.

The shaft must now be held in a vice, with suitable clamps shaped to suit the tube size (this is most important to avoid damage to the shaft) and the sleeve nut at the lower end unscrewed, for which a ring spanner is strongly recommended. The shaft is thickest at about six inches from the top and this is the portion that should be gripped in the vice. To remove the oil-seal, service tool Part No. 61-3006 is required and when a new seal is being fitted into the sleeve it must be inserted with the lip downwards. This will require service tool Part No. 61-3007.

Examine the bushes and sliding tube for wear, replacing as thought fit. When reassembling, tighten the bottom sleeve nut really firmly, and on no account omit the circlip from the upper bush. Before the sleeve and its oil-seal is screwed home, add one turn of twine into the undercut at the end of the thread to make an additional oil-seal.

To refit the fork shaft, insert service tool Part No. 61-3350 into the thread at the taper end and feed it through the lower yoke and into the upper one. Add the collar and nut, and draw the shaft fully home into its taper seat. Tighten the clip bolt on the lower steering stem yoke and remove the service tool. Replenish the fork legs with the correct amount of oil (*see* page 94) and replace the cap nut.

FIG. 54.
DISMANTLING THE FORK OIL-SEAL

250 STAR. Three service tools are required for dismantling these forks and as at least one of them is expensive, it may be preferable for a B.S.A. dealer to carry out the work, but for those who wish to do the job for themselves the following notes will prove to be of some assistance.

The fork shafts are clamped into the lower steering yoke and when these bolts have been removed, unscrew the cap nut A (*see* Fig. 51). Service tool Part No. 61-3350 (Fig. 55) should now be screwed into the internal thread in the top of the fork shaft and its end struck a sharp blow with a hammer, thus freeing the shaft from its taper seat in the top steering yoke, allowing it to be drawn downwards through the bottom yoke. Withdraw the spring.

The collar at the upper end of the sliding tube is next to be removed. Grip the wheel-spindle lug in a vice (not the tube, otherwise it may be

STEERING AND SUSPENSION

distorted) and unscrew the collar with the aid of service tool Part No. 61-3586 although, in this case, a suitable "cee" spanner may do the job equally well. Pressed into the upper part of the collar is a sleeve carrying two oil-seals spaced about $1\frac{1}{2}$ in. apart, the lower one being retained between the sleeve and the collar. If these seals have shown signs of being faulty, new ones must be inserted with the spring-loaded lip downwards.

To dismantle the fork still further for renewal of the bushes, the restrictor rod in the centre of the sliding tube must be taken out. It is attached by a bolt accessible from the wheel-spindle lug, and will require a socket spanner to unscrew it. When free, the rod will fall out of the shaft if the latter is turned upside down. Here it should be noted that there is a slot at the taper end of the restrictor rod, and when this is replaced, the slot must be fitted over the drain screw which projects into the sliding tube.

To separate the fixed and sliding tubes it is necessary to use service tool Part No. 61-3587, because the upper bearing is a tight fit in the sliding tube and a certain amount of force is required to move it. The sliding tube must be bolted to the end plate of the tool, using two of the wheel-spindle lug bolts, so that the fork shaft, complete with bush and spacer sleeve, can be drawn out together. The lower bush on the shaft can be removed after unscrewing the ring nut. This also will require the use of a "cee" spanner, while the shaft is held in a vice, using suitable clamps.

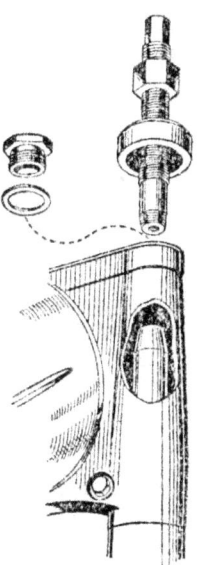

FIG. 55. FORK LEG REPLACEMENT TOOL

The same tool is used for dismantling.

Examine the bushes and sliding tubes and, having decided upon renewals, reassembly can commence. Replace the lower bush on the fork shaft and tighten the ring nut securely. Slide the spacing sleeve, and top bush (flange uppermost) onto the fixed shaft, and insert the latter into the sliding member, lower bush first. The spacer sleeve and top bush can be driven into position with a piece of tubing, of such length and bore that it will fit over the shaft. Take care not to damage the top face of the bush. Next screw on the collar complete with sleeve and oil-seals and as it is moved down the shaft into position take the greatest care to ensure that the oil-seal lips are not damaged or turned back, as this will cause oil leakage. Tighten with service tool Part No. 61-3586. Insert the restrictor rod and, using the spring as a locator, fit the rod in position over the drain screw and screw up its fixing bolt. Withdraw the spring and slide the fork shaft up through the bottom steering yoke into the top yoke, and insert the service tool into the thread in the shaft. Add the collar and nut, and draw the shaft into its taper seat in the top yoke.

With the tool still in position, tighten the shaft clamp bolts in the bottom steering yoke and then remove the tool. Replenish the forks with the correct amount of oil (*see* page 94) and replace the spring followed by the cap nut.

Following the reassembly of the mudguard, when assembling the wheel, special attention should be given to the method of replacement as detailed on page 36. As soon as the support has been removed from beneath the engine and the machine is on its wheels again, slacken the wheel-spindle lug bolts and align the fork shafts as described on page 36.

BARRACUDA AND STARFIRE MODELS. Remove the front-fork shafts as described for the 250 Star, but note that before the cap nut A, (Fig. 51) can be removed, it must be raised sufficiently for the lock-nut (on the rod below it) to be slackened. On the 1968 Starfire model only, as the shaft is withdrawn, the rubber bellows can be left in position on the shroud. With the spring withdrawn, unscrew the oil-seal holder, using Service tool No. 61–3005 as shown in Fig. 54 and slide the holder upwards until it tightens on to the tapered portion of the shaft. Do not use force here, otherwise the seal may be damaged. The shaft and lower sliding member can now be separated. The bush in the sliding member may be tight, and appreciable effort may be required to withdraw it.

Holding the upper end (unground portion) of the shaft in a vice fitted with lead clamps, unscrew the large nut at the opposite end, so thereby releasing the bushes, spacer, and oil seal assembly. The damper tube is retained at its base by a socket-head screw and after this, plus the two circlips at the top of the tube, is taken out, the damper-rod assembly can be dismantled.

If the oil seal is faulty it can be driven out of its holder with Service tool No. 61–3006. A new seal should be greased at its feather edge before assembly and have its *outside* diameter coated with jointing compound. Drive the new seal squarely into the holder while still wet, using Service tool No. 61–3007. Examine the bushes for wear, renewing bushes as required.

When reassembling the fork shaft on the sliding member, little effort should be required to fit the long bush. Then tighten the oil-seal holder on to one turn of twine at the base of the screw thread to form a further oil seal.

Reassembly of the fork shaft requires the use of Service tool No. 61–3350 to draw it firmly into the tapered hole in the yoke. Lock the clamp bolts in the lower yoke before removing the tool. Raise the damper rod to the top of the shaft with Service tool No. 61–3765, fit the cap nut and secure with its lock-nut. Do not omit the seal and its retainer below the lock-nut. Add oil as recommended on page 94 and screw down the cap nuts firmly. Replacement of the mudguard, front wheel, etc., now completes the operation.

STARFIRE (1969–70). While retaining an overall similarity with the previous year, the front forks on these models are of different construction internally, particularly as far as the damping unit is concerned. This comprises a simple shuttle valve at the lower end of the fork stanchion,

STEERING AND SUSPENSION

together with a restrictor rod secured at the base of the sliding member

Removal of the complete fork leg has already been described for earlier Starfires, and remains the same for later models, following which the rubber gaiter and suspension spring may be removed.

From this point, to dismantle the fork leg, hold the sliding member by its wheel spindle lug and unscrew the oil seal holder using Service tool No. 61-6017 (right-hand thread). The stanchion, complete with lower bush, shuttle, etc., can then be drawn out of the sliding member, bringing with it the upper bush, which is a light press-fit in that member. (A few sharp jerks may be necessary here, more especially if the upper bush is fitted a little tightly.) The lower bush and shuttle on the stanchion are together retained by a special nut which requires the use of a "C" shaped spanner for removal. The shuttle is released after extracting its circlip. The restrictor is retained in the sliding member and its securing bolt is accessible through the wheel spindle lug.

If the oil seal is to be removed, it can be driven out from the threaded end of its holder by means of a hammer and a flat-headed punch. The new seal must be inserted with its lip towards the thread of the holder. At the same time, check that the internal rubber "O" ring is still serviceable.

When reassembling, a study of the illustration, Fig. 55A, will do much to simplify assembly of the fork leg.

If difficulty is experienced in replacing the restrictor, this will be simplified by first placing in the shuttle valve (after this has been reassembled to the stanchion) and then using the valve as a guide to locate the restrictor in its hole in the base of the outer member.

Slide the assembled stanchion into the bottom member and fit the inner sleeve, top bush, and outer washer. Screw on the oil seal assembly and tighten down with the Service tool.

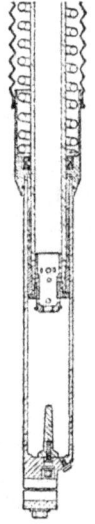

FIG. 55A. SECTION THROUGH THE FRONT FORK-LEG. 1969-70 STARFIRE

Re-fitting the legs to the top yoke will require, first, the use of Service tool No. 61-3824 to draw the stanchion into its taper seat, and then the temporary tightening of the leg pinch bolts in the bottom yoke. Remove the tool and replace with the cap nut which can be fully tightened following the slackening of the lower pinch bolts.

At this stage it will be advisable to make any adjustment to the steering head bearings (see page 91), following which the pinch bolts may be re-tightened fully.

When reassembly is completed, replenish the fork legs with the correct quantity of oil (page 94), of a suitable grade (page 4).

7 The Electrical Equipment

ALL B.S.A. 250 c.c. machines utilize an alternator mounted on the engine shaft, as the means of generating electricity for charging the battery.

Unlike a dynamo, there are no moving parts in contact with each other, so that the alternator requires no maintenance other than an occasional examination to see that the air-gap between rotor and stator is being maintained. If at any time the engine is dismantled it is not necessary to fit "keepers" to the poles of the rotor.

Output from the alternator is changed from a.c. to d.c. current by passing through a rectifier, and varies automatically according to requirements.

This increased output is also used for starting the engine in an emergency such as when the battery may have become discharged. On all C10L, C11G and C12 machines the ignition switch takes the form of a detachable key mounted in the centre of the lighting switch and to obtain the emergency position, the key must be depressed and turned anti-clockwise. The 250 Star carries the ignition switch on the centre panel behind the engine and in the case of the earlier models there is no separate key, the emergency or the main position being obtained by a turn of the knob. On 250 Stars, from engine No. 29838, and Sport Stars (SS80) from engine No. 1101, a detachable key is incorporated which operates in the same manner as already described. As soon as the ignition switch is moved to the emergency position, the output from the generator passes to the ignition coil, and the battery also receives a charging current. After the engine has been started under these conditions, the ignition switch should be moved sharply to its normal position, when the battery will receive its normal charging current. Failure to do this may cause misfiring, serving as a reminder to move the switch to its correct position.

Circumstances may arise where the charging rate is insufficient, such as continuous low-speed running, and on Lucas equipment it is possible to increase the charging rate from the alternator by interchanging the cables at their snap connectors, as follows—On earlier models interchange the Dark Green and Medium Green cables; on later models, the Dark Green is interchanged with the Green-Yellow cable, and on still later models the Green-Black cable should be interchanged with Green-Yellow. Examination of the cables will show which of these colours applies to your machine. If normal running is resumed, the original connexions should be made, otherwise the battery may receive an excessive charging rate (denoted by the need for frequent topping-up).

THE ELECTRICAL EQUIPMENT 105

Barracuda and Starfire Equipment. For the first time on B.S.A. 250 c.c. motor-cycles, these recent models have 12-volt lighting and ignition systems. A zener-diode controls the charge rate to the battery from a generator which is continuously delivering its full output, and hence the battery is always fully charged under normal running conditions. Surplus energy is dissipated in the form of heat via a "heat sink" mounted under the steering head.

The generator output is sufficient to enable a start to be made with a discharged battery and consequently an "emergency start" switch position is unnecessary. A detachable ignition key is located on the frame at the front of the dualseat.

Batteries. These must never be left in a discharged condition, otherwise the plates will suffer harm. If the battery is not to be used for, say, two or three weeks, charge it from an external source and give a short charge at fortnightly intervals. All the a.c. equipment on the various models has been designed for "positive-earth" (+) and if the battery is connected wrongly, the rectifier and other items will be damaged. The positive (+) lead from the battery *must* be connected to the frame.

LUCAS ML9E. This battery is fitted to the 250 c.c. Star model only and as the body is of translucent material, the level of the electrolyte can be seen readily. A coloured line embodied in the battery shows the maximum level for the electrolyte and this must never be exceeded. Owing to the compact nature of this battery, the level should be checked at weekly intervals, but it is not possible to use the normal type of battery filler, or to use a hydrometer to check the specific gravity of the electrolyte. Use distilled water only.

LUCAS PUZ5E (12 VOLTS). This battery, used on the Barracuda and Starfire machines requires the same attention as the Lucas ML9E just referred to.

VARLEY. Whilst these batteries have the same general characteristics as a lead-acid battery, there are also important differences in construction which require a departure from the normal topping-up procedure. A porous material occupies the space between the plates, and completely absorbs all the acid, and hence there should not be any free acid in the battery. Normally, a teaspoonful of distilled water is sufficient for topping-up, at monthly intervals, to replace the fluid lost by evaporation and electrolysis. All the added liquid should be absorbed within about a quarter of an hour, when any surplus must be syphoned out, otherwise there may be an overflow. It is not possible to use a hydrometer with these batteries and the state of charge can be determined by the voltage under load, which should be a minimum of 6·3 volts when fully charged. It is not advisable to top-up immediately before a journey.

OTHER LUCAS BATTERIES. At intervals of about a fortnight, unscrew the filler plugs and examine the level of the electrolyte. If necessary, add distilled water until the electrolyte is just above the top of the separators. A battery filler will automatically ensure the correct level.

Later types of battery incorporate devices in each cell which ensure correct electrolyte level without the use of a special filler, and these devices (usually consisting of a perforated flange fitted with a central tube) must be used conscientiously. Add distilled water round the flange until no more will drain through, and lift the tube slightly to clear the remaining water, when the level will be correct.

The specific gravity of the electrolyte can be checked, if required, with a small volume hydrometer, but it may be necessary to tilt the battery in order to obtain sufficient electrolyte for the operation.

Zener-diode. Used on the Barracuda and Starfire models only, this item does not normally require any attention, but if it is disturbed at any time, the torque applied when tightening must not exceed 24/28 lb. ins.

Rectifier. This does not require maintenance, but if it is disturbed for any reason take care to distinguish between the nut holding the rectifier to the frame and the nut locking the plates together. If the latter nut is slackened, the performance of the rectifier will be adversely affected.

Ignition Coil. Maintenance is unnecessary beyond keeping the surface between the terminals clean and checking that the terminals themselves are clean.

The Contact-breaker Unit. Adjustment of the contact-breaker, together with its associated auto-advance and retard mechanism, is normally carried out as part of the engine maintenance (page 14). If the points are blackened or burnt, clean with a fine carborundum stone, afterwards wiping with a cloth moistened in petrol. Apply a thin smear of grease to the cam. Avoid excessive lubrication.

Setting the Headlamp Beam. To obtain the best visibility shine the lamp onto a smooth, light-coloured wall at a distance of about 25 ft. when the centre of the area of concentrated light should be at the same height above the ground as the centre of the lamp. Note particularly that the machine should be normally loaded when this check is being made. The complete lamp can be tilted in the case of machines with separate headlamps, but with the 250 c.c. Star, the three screws securing the headlamp rim must first be slackened, and the light unit moved until the above condition is obtained.

Warning Light. On Barracuda and Starfire models prior to 1969 (see page 114) an added refinement is a red warning light on the headlamp which indicates when the main beam is in use. The colour becomes green or blue, on 1969–70 Starfires.

Stop Light. On most models, movement of the rear brake pedal actuates a switch, controlling the stop-light. The switch operation should be checked whenever the pedal position is adjusted.

THE ELECTRICAL EQUIPMENT

For 1969-70 Starfires only, a stop-light switch is also incorporated in the front brake cable. This switch does not require any adjustment or attention.

Bulb Replacement. In all cases it is necessary to remove the rim of the lamp to gain access to the bulbs.

On model C10L it is necessary only to bend back the locking tab securing the bulb-holder bracket and turn it anti-clockwise, when both pilot and main bulbs can be removed. When replacing the main bulb (6 volt, 30/30 watt) make sure that the dip filament, i.e. the offset filament, is uppermost. Do not attempt to clean the surface of the reflector which will be harmed by the use of normal cleaning materials.

Other headlamps with a self-contained light unit carry the main bulb in a detachable holder of the bayonet fixing type. Depress the holder and turn anti-clockwise to release the bulb (6 volt, 30/24 watt). The latter is of the pre-focus type and is constructed so that it cannot be replaced with the filaments the wrong way round. The carrier of the pilot bulb (6 volt, 3 watt) is a push-fit in the reflector.

Access to the tail-light bulb is simply obtained by removing the lens retaining screws, except on the early C10L machines, where the lamp cover is retained by a bayonet fitting. For the C10L machine, the bulb is 6 volt, 6 watt, with 6 volt, 3 watt stop-light bulbs, or 6 volt, 3/18 watt, with combined stop-tail light bulb. All other tail lamps use a combined stop-tail light bulb of 6 volt, 6/18 watt.

For 12 volt equipment the current bulbs are: Headlamp—12 volt, 50/40 watt; Main beam warning light—24 volt, 2 watt; Pilot bulb—12 volt, 6 watt; stop-tail lamp—12 volt, 6/21 watt.

Fuse. On the 1968-70 Starfires only, a 35 amp fuse is fitted in the feed line adjacent to the battery. Press the ends together and twist to release the fuse cartridge.

Wiring Diagrams. Diagrams for the various models appear in the following pages.

Capacitor. Provision is made on 1969-70 models for the fitting of a capacitor, which enables the engine to be run without the battery, and hence is suitable for most emergencies concerning ignition and lighting. When the engine is running all lighting is available, but the parking lights cannot be used when the engine is stationary. To run with the battery disconnected, its negative lead must be insulated from the frame to prevent short-circuiting, otherwise the capacitor will be ruined.

If a capacitor is fitted, check its serviceability at intervals by disconnecting the battery, when the engine should continue to run normally.

A kit of parts, together with assembly instructions, is obtainable from the B.S.A. Spares Dept. under part No. 00-4403.

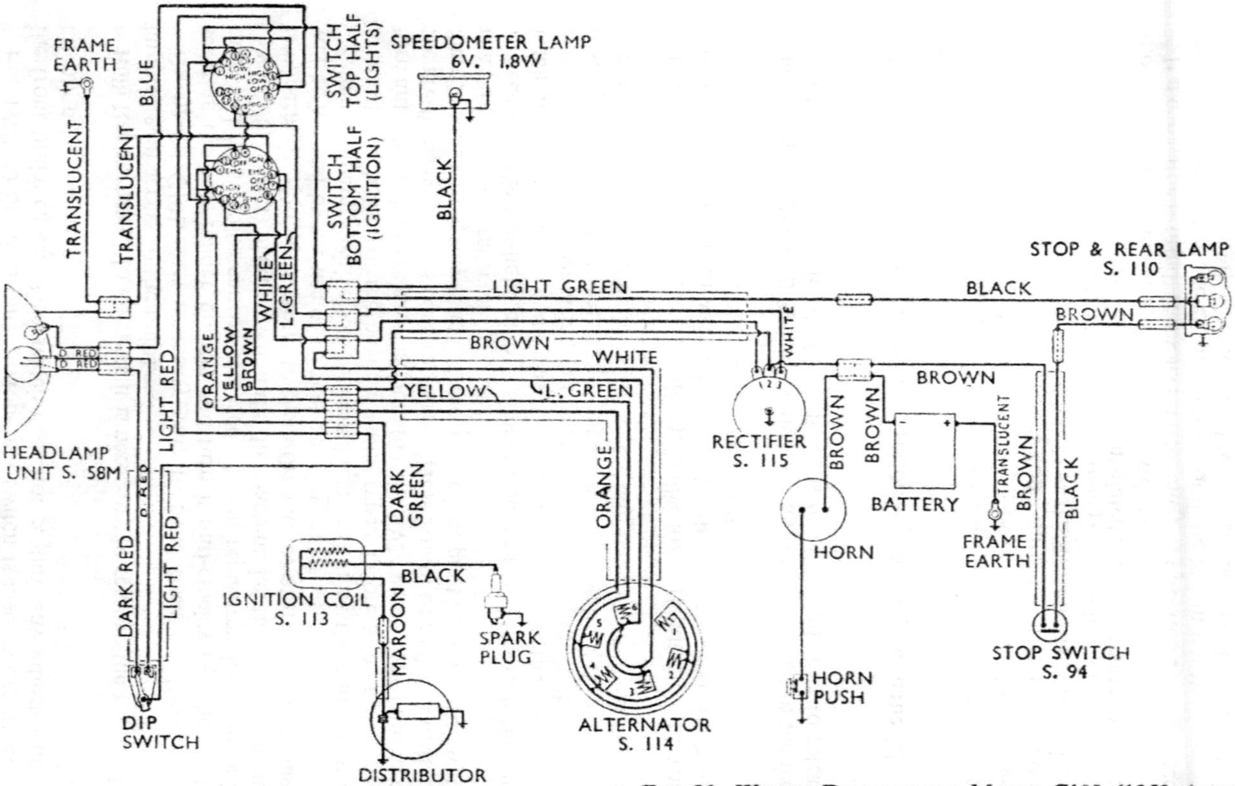

FIG. 56. WIRING DIAGRAM FOR MODEL C10L (1953–AUGUST 1954)

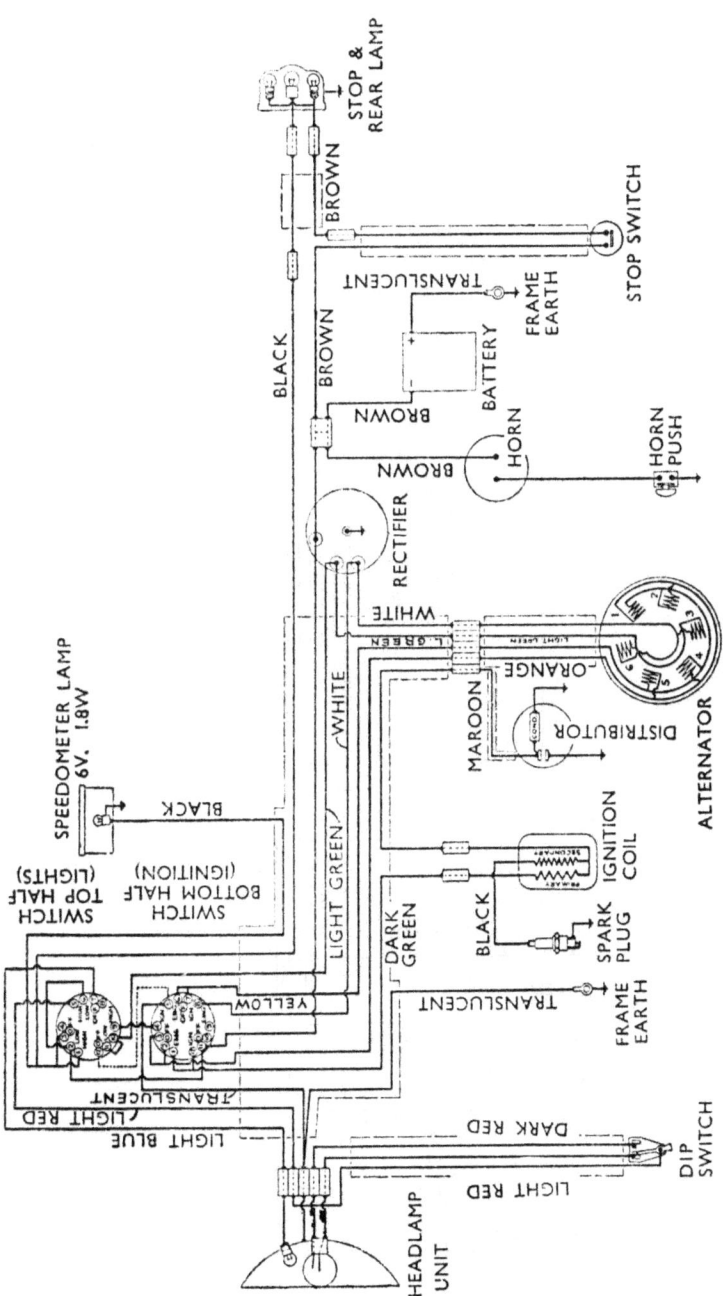

Fig. 57. Wiring Diagram for Model C10L (October 1954–July 1955), with link between No. 12 (top) and No. 5 (bottom) should have the connexion removed as shown by the dotted line.

Note that switches supplied from approximately October 1, 1954 to January 1955.

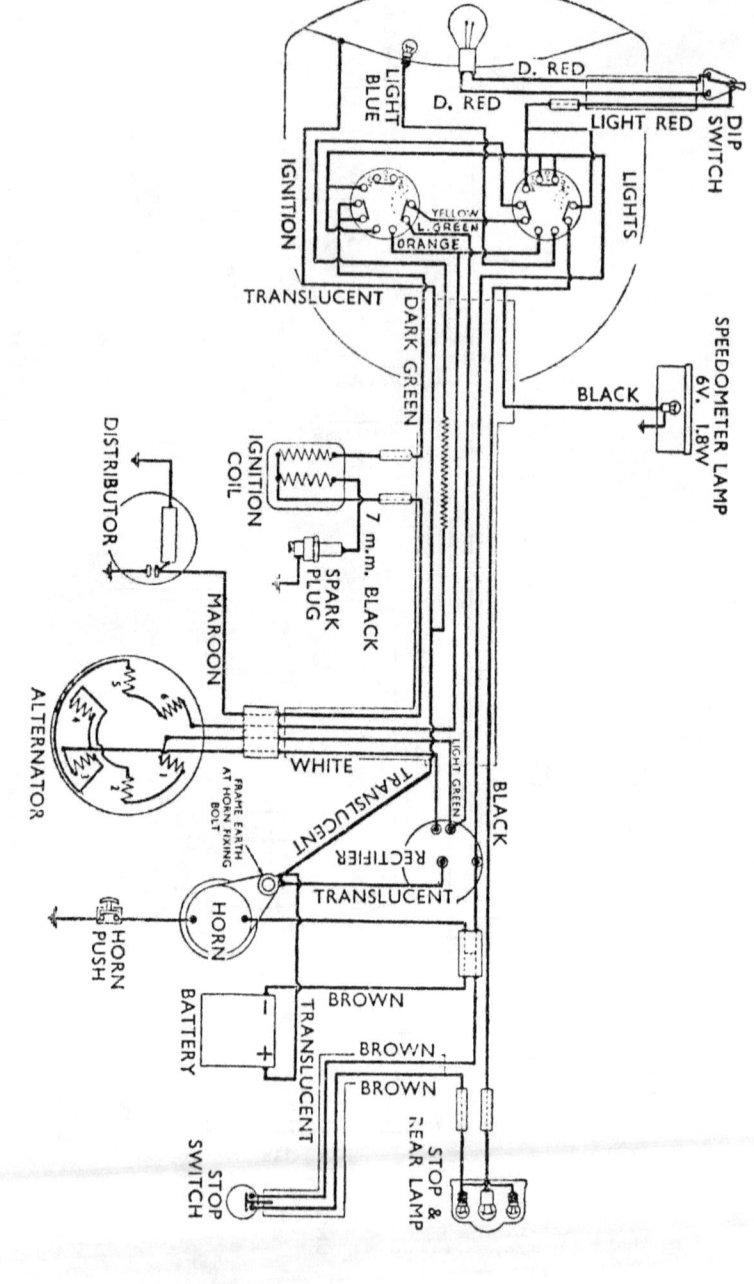

Fig. 58. Wiring Diagram for Model C10L (as from August, 1955)

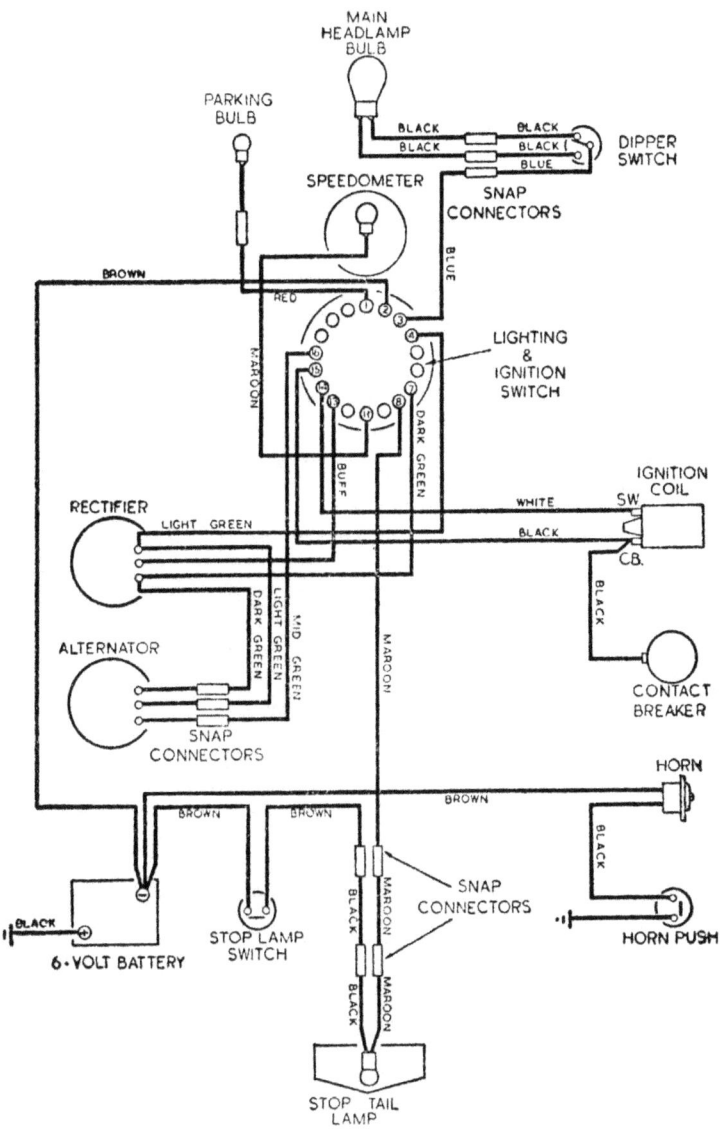

FIG. 59. WIRING DIAGRAM FOR MODEL C11G

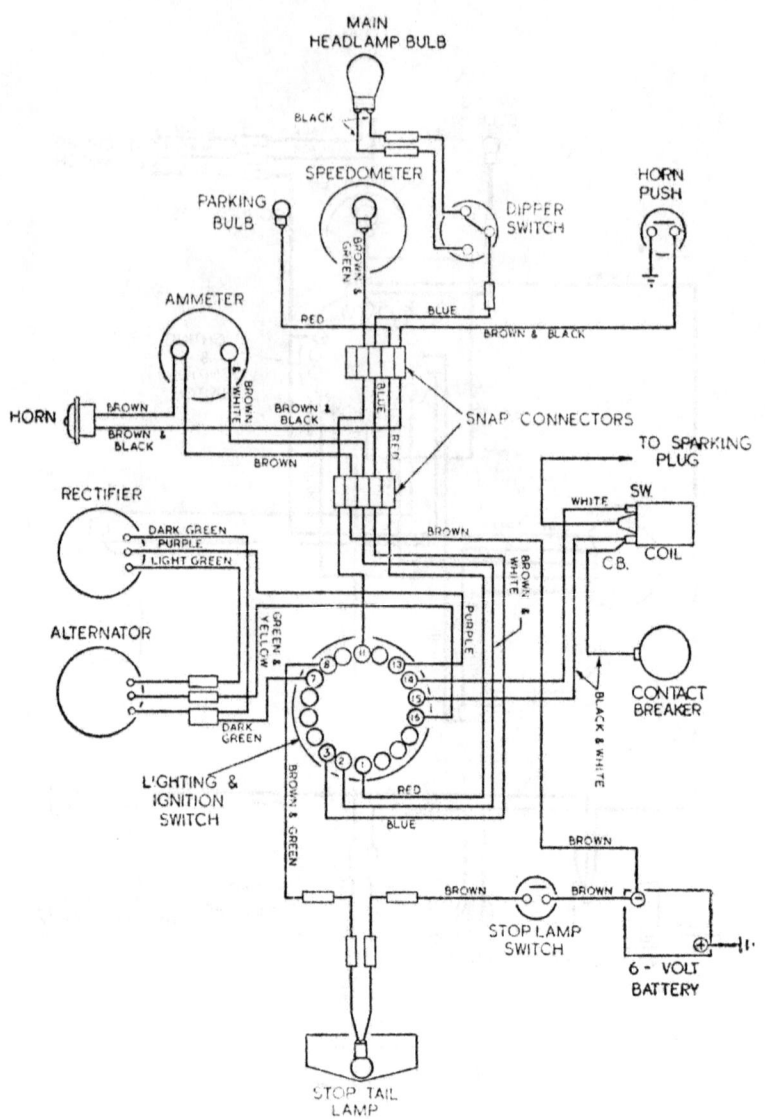

Fig. 60. Wiring Diagram for Model C12

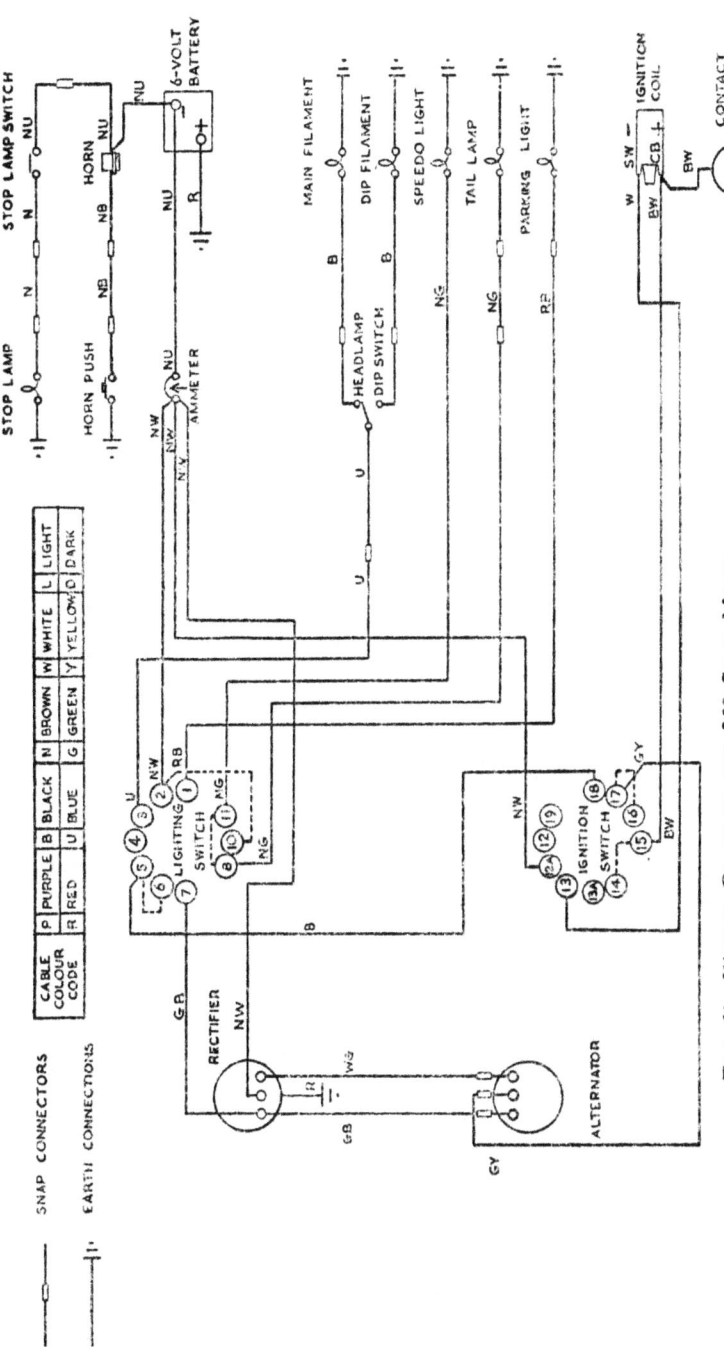

FIG. 61. WIRING DIAGRAM FOR 250 STAR MODEL

For models made after 1964, the circuit is similar to the above except for an additional lead from the rectifier *WG* lead to position 4 of the lighting switch, and the stop lamp and switch are connected to the *W* cable from the ignition coil. Headlamp main beam lead is *UW* and the dip beam lead is *UR*, the lead from bulb to earth being *R*.

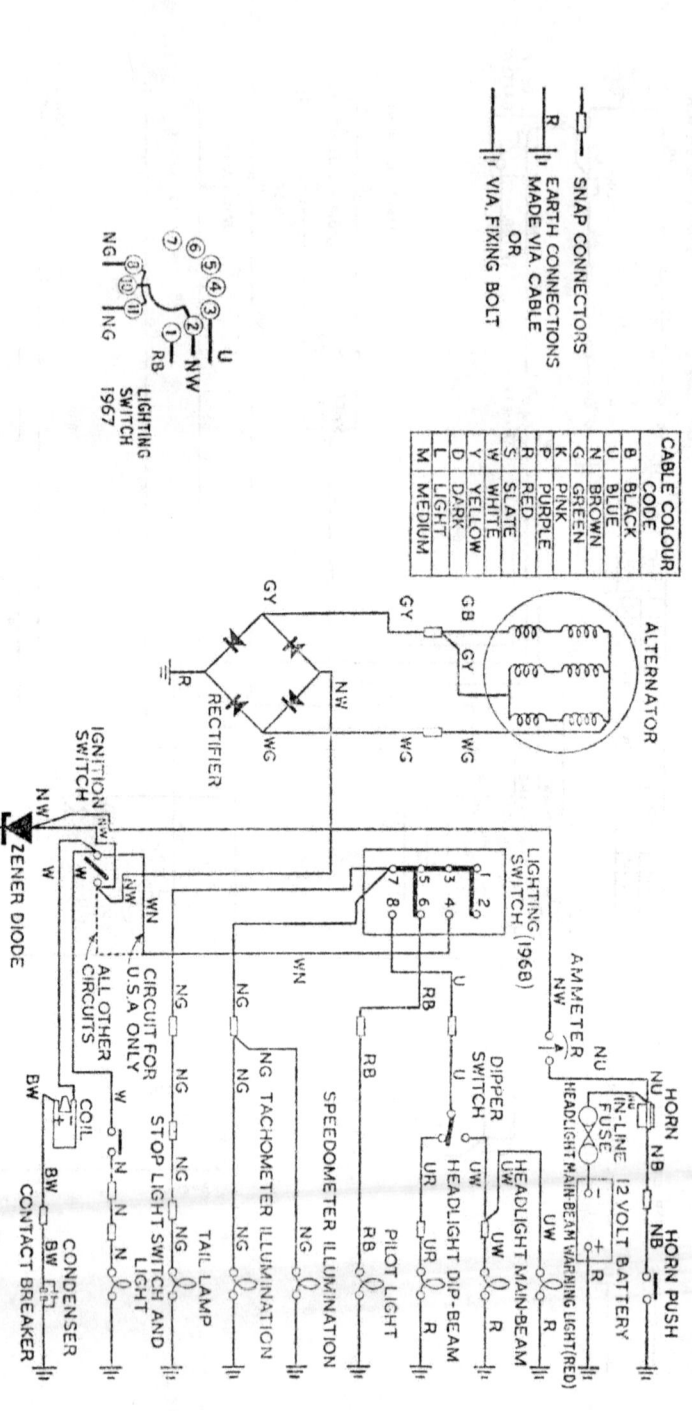

FIG. 62. WIRING DIAGRAM FOR 1967–70 BARRACUDA AND STARFIRE MODELS

The lighting switch shown in the diagram for 1968, continues for 1969–70. Specified on 1970 models only, the oil pressure switch and its associated red warning light are coupled in series to the "W" terminal of the ignition switch. The headlamp main beam warning light is changed to green (blue on some models).

8 The Carburettor

THE function of a carburettor is to vaporize the petrol and provide a correct ratio of air and petrol to the engine. The actual operation of the carburettor is simple, there are few adjustments to be made, and these can be easily carried out by the private owner. All the carburettors on 250 c.c. B.S.A. machines are similar in principle, the main difference being, that on the older models the float chamber is a separate unit, whereas on the later

TABLE IV. CARBURETTOR SETTINGS

Model	Main Jet	Main Jet with Cleaner	Throttle Slide	Needle Position	Needle Jet
C10L	90	—	4/4	2	0·1055
C10L (Monobloc)	120	85	3½	2	0·1055
C11G	80	—	4/4	3	0·1055
C11G (Monobloc)	140	100	3½	3	0·1055
C15	—	140	4	3	0·1055
C15 (SS80) Sportsman	—	200	4	2	0·106
Barracuda Starfire	—	200	3	2	0·107
Starfire (1969–70)	—	170	3	1	0·106

version (the "Monobloc") the float chamber is incorporated in the body of the carburettor, whilst the jet positions have also been changed in the later type. Normally, the owner will be concerned with two items connected with his carburettor—petrol consumption and power output. A new machine as received from the makers will have the best settings of needle position, main jet, etc., suitable for his machine and these should not be experimented with in any way. On other than new machines, however, it will be as well to verify the carburettor settings and these are given in Table IV. The fitting of an air cleaner usually requires a change in main jet, as the cleaner slightly restricts the flow of air through the carburettor and consequently a similar restriction is necessary to the main jet to keep the air-petrol ratio the same, i.e. a smaller one must be used. This is also a very good reason for keeping the air cleaner itself clean, otherwise the normal jet setting will give a rich mixture and therefore an increase in petrol consumption. The 250 Star, Barracuda, and Starfire models are supplied with an air cleaner as a standard fitment, but on the other models an air cleaner was an extra and jet sizes for use with and without a cleaner are therefore quoted.

In the above table, the needle position is expressed as the number of the groove from the top of the needle which carries its fixing clip. The throttle

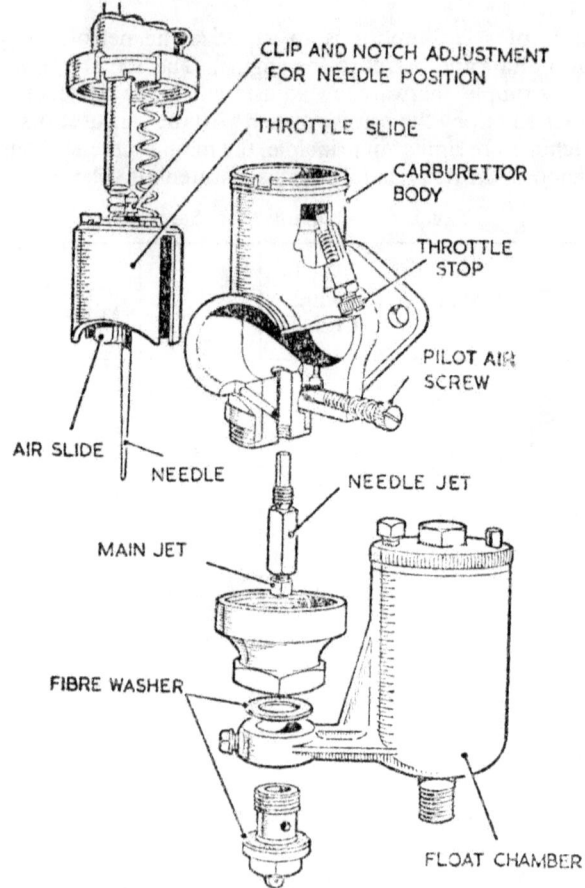

FIG. 63. AMAL STANDARD CARBURETTOR, SHOWN PARTLY DISMANTLED, AS FITTED TO 1954 MODELS ONLY

slide is the cylindrical sleeve to which the needle is attached, whilst the needle jet is the long jet in which the lower end of the needle slides. The needle is gently tapered, so that, as the throttle slide position varies (by cable from the twist-grip control) the needle position in the needle jet varies and hence the effective aperture size changes accordingly, so varying the flow of petrol to the engine. The needle jet is of a predetermined size, but if worn (as it may be after a considerable mileage), it must be replaced, otherwise the petrol consumption will suffer. It will be noted that the throttle slide is cut away at an angle and this affects the petrol-to-air ratio of the carburettor between the stages of running on the pilot jet and the needle jet range. The air slide (the smaller of the two) is used for cold starting or with a cold engine, when it is normally closed or partly closed. At normal engine temperatures it should be wide open (i.e. raised to its limit).

The purpose of the float chamber is to ensure a correct level of fuel at the jets and to cut off the supply from the tank when the level has risen to its correct height. It is usually necessary to use a rich mixture for starting purposes and for this reason the carburettor has to be flooded. This means preventing the float from rising normally and for this purpose a spring-loaded plunger (familiarly known as the "tickler") is fitted to the float chamber. To flood the carburettor the tickler should be depressed for a few seconds (not jabbed rapidly for fear of damage to the float), when petrol may be seen dripping from the carburettor. It is unnecessary to flood the carburettor when the engine is hot, as a normal mixture is sufficient. If the carburettor is of the single-lever type, i.e. there is no air-control lever, it will be essential to flood the carburettor more or less, according to the engine temperature. The amount will have to be determined by experiment.

On carburettors with a separate float chamber, the float carries a sharply tapered needle which rises and falls off its seating according to the petrol level, thus controlling the flow of fuel. With machines which have seen considerable use the taper portion may have become worn so allowing the float to rise a little and hence the petrol level will be permanently too high. This may lead to continual slight flooding with, of course, an increase in fuel consumption. In such an event the needle should be replaced: it is retained by a clip above the float. After slackening the locking screw, the float chamber cover may be unscrewed, to expose the float and its clip. Squeeze the clip ends together and draw the float upwards leaving the needle in position. The needle can then be taken out by unscrewing the needle seating from below the chamber. When reassembling, make sure that the float clip is securely in position in the groove on the needle. In the case of the Monobloc carburettor, the float is hinged at one side and raises or lowers the tapered needle near the hinge of the float. Access to these parts is obtained by removing the side cover. The washer here must always be in good condition to ensure a petrol-tight joint.

The main jet is exposed when the cap nut is removed from below the carburettor, an action which will also free the float chamber where this is a separate unit. This jet is calibrated to give a precise discharge and the hole must never be modified in any way. A replacement jet will have the same calibration number marked on its top face.

Projecting at an angle from the carburettor body is the throttle-slide

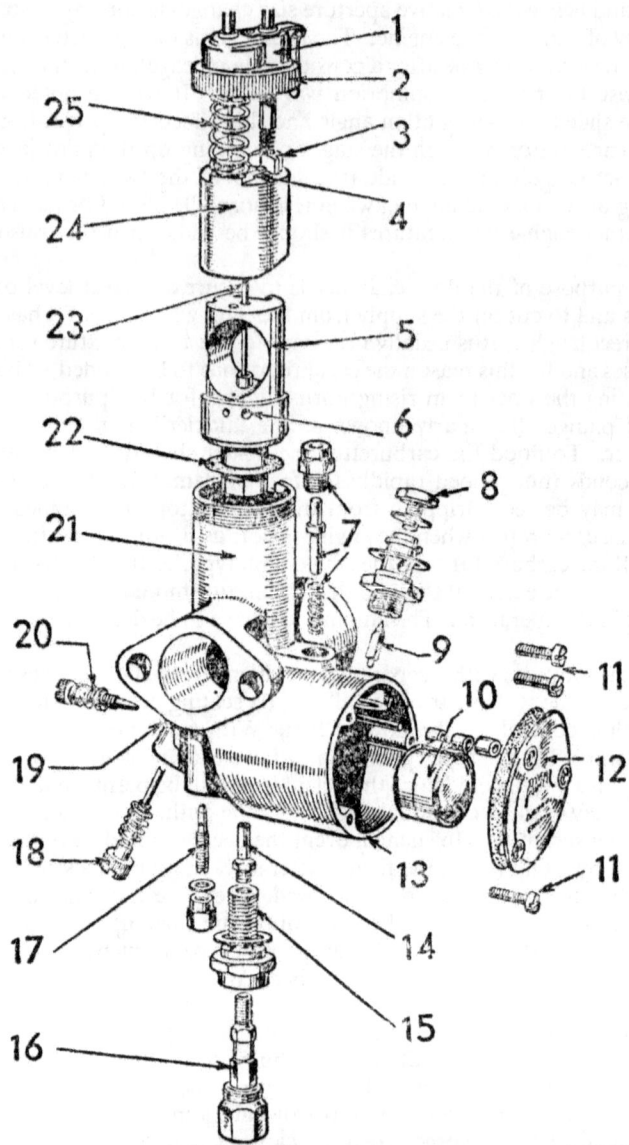

Fig. 64. Exploded View of Amal "Monobloc" Carburettor
On the Sportsman and SS80 Sports Star, an air slide is fitted as shown.
Key on facing page.

THE CARBURETTOR

stop screw and its purpose is to keep the slide open by an amount sufficient to keep the engine running slowly when the twist-grip is closed. A lock nut retains it in position. The spring-loaded screw projecting horizontally from the carburettor body controls the amount of air feeding to the pilot jet, and so regulates the mixture at "tick-over," and for the initial throttle opening.

There are two main faults which can develop in carburation—the mixture can be either too rich or too weak. If too rich, one or more of the following symptoms should be noticed—heavy petrol consumption; black smoke in the exhaust (absurdly rich, possibly due to a closed air slide or heavy flooding); eight-stroking (i.e. the engine firing regularly but at half its normal frequency); sparking plug sooty (distinguish here between a surface which is sooty or covered in burnt oil), air cleaner choked; "lumpy" running of the engine.

With a weak mixture, the signs would be—spitting back in the carburettor; erratic slow running; overheating; engine performance improving if air slide is partially closed; grey deposit at the sparking plug points.

Air leaks will also give a weak mixture, and cause erratic slow running. A likely cause is a faulty joint between the carburettor and the engine. Pour a little oil over the joint when the engine is running and if a leak is present the oil will be drawn in. Fit new joint washer. Worn inlet valve guides will also produce the same effect. Similarly, explosions in the exhaust are usually an indication of too weak a pilot mixture, but on the other hand it could be too rich a pilot mixture, coupled with a leak in the exhaust system.

Tuning the Carburettor. When tuning the carburettor, always follow the same sequence as that here given and do not start until the engine has obtained its normal running temperature. The air slide must be kept fully open throughout the operations unless instructed otherwise.

Main Jet. This controls the supply of petrol to the engine when the throttle control is not less than three-quarters open. Run the engine at full speed. If the performance is better with the air control closed slightly, or with the twist-grip eased back a little, the jet is too small. If the engine runs roughly, the jet is too large.

Pilot Jet. When the throttle control is up to one-eighth open, the pilot jet is responsible for the mixture passing to the engine. Slacken the

Key to Fig. 64

1. Mixing-chamber cap
2. Mixing-chamber cap ring
3. Air slide
4. Jet-needle clip
5. Jet block
6. Air passage to pilot jet
7. Tickler assembly
8. Banjo securing-bolt
9. Float needle
10. Float
11. Float-chamber cover screws
12. Float-chamber cover
13. Float chamber
14. Needle jet
15. Main-jet holder
16. Main jet
17. Pilot jet
18. Throttle-stop adjusting screw
19. Jet block locating screw
20. Pilot air-adjusting screw
21. Mixing chamber
22. Fibre seal
23. Jet needle
24. Throttle slide
25. Throttle return-spring

throttle slide screw and lower the slide until the engine falters and then adjust the pilot air screw until the engine runs regularly, also a little faster. Repeat this procedure two or three times until the best slow-running is obtained.

Throttle Slide. The "cut-away" in this slide controls the next phase of the throttle opening, i.e. from one-eighth to a quarter open. If opening the twist-grip causes spitting from the carburettor, screw in the pilot air screw by a small amount (say half-a-turn) to enrich the mixture. If this does not

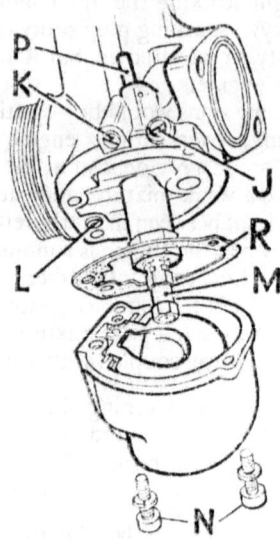

FIG. 65. PARTLY DISMANTLED AMAL CONCENTRIC CARBURETTOR

affect a cure, return the pilot air screw to its previous position and fit another throttle slide with the next smaller "cut away." Alternatively, if the engine runs irregularly under load at this throttle position without spitting, a larger "cut-away" is required, or the throttle needle is too high.

Throttle Needle. This controls the widest range of throttle opening (from a quarter to three-quarters open) and also the acceleration. Check with the needle in the lowest position when the clip will be in the uppermost groove. If the acceleration is poor and better results are obtained with the air slide partly closed, raise the needle by two grooves. If the improvement is most marked, lower the needle one more notch and check again, leaving it finally in the position which gives the best acceleration.

It may be that the mixture is still too rich with the clip in the uppermost groove and this means that the needle jet needs to be replaced due to wear. The needle will require renewing only after a very long life.

THE CARBURETTOR

Finally, having made all these adjustments it is a good plan to check that the idling is still satisfactory.

BARRACUDA AND STARFIRE

The Amal "Concentric" Carburettor. Fig. 65 shows the Amal carburettor fitted to Barracuda and Starfire models. It is similar in operation, tuning, etc., to the Monobloc type, differing only in construction.

The float chamber is mounted concentrically with the main body (hence the name) and must be dismounted at screws N (Fig. 65) before the main and pilot jets are accessible shown at M and L respectively). During this operation take great care of the float and the gasket R. If either is damaged it must be renewed.

The throttle slide stop-screw K and pilot-air screw J are retained by rubber rings to prevent unintentional slackening.

Starfire (1969-70). A modification in design of the carburettor dispenses with the detachable pilot jet L, which now takes the form of a bush cast in position. It is not detachable and the only adjustment which can be made to the pilot mixture is by means of the pilot air screw.

Index

AIR cleaner, 27
Auto-advance mechanism, 17
BATTERY, 105
Big-end replacement, 75, 81
Brake adjustment, 33
Brake shoe replacement, 34
CARBURETTOR, 115
Chain—
  adjustment,
    primary, 28
    rear, 31
  lubrication,
    front, 8
    rear, 9
  wear, 30
Clutch—
  access to, 43
  adjustment, 41
  removal, 46
  spring pressure, 44
Clutch plate removal, 44
Clutch shock absorber, 45
Contact breaker, 106
Cylinder barrel, 72
Cylinder head—
  gasket, 67
  removal, 67
  replacement, 76
DECARBONIZING, 66
ELECTRICAL equipment, 104
Engine—
  dismantling, 78
  reassembling, 82, 86
FILTERS, 6
Forks, 94, 98
GEARBOXES—
  four-speed, 57
    light, 50
    unit construction, 61

GEARBOXES (*contd.*)—
  lubrication, 9
  three-speed, 53
HEADLAMP—
  beam setting, 106
  bulb replacement, 107
IGNITION coil, 106
LITTLE end, 74
Lubricating system, 1
Lubrication, general, 8
PISTON, 72
REAR light bulb replacement, 107
Rectifier, 106
Rings, 73
SPARKING plug, 22
Steering head, 91
Suspension, 94–5
Swinging-arm, 96
TIMING—
  ignition, 19
  valve, 23
Tuning the carburettor, 119
VALVE—
  clearances, 11
  grinding, 70
  guides, 69
  removing, 68
  replacing, 70
  springs, 70
Valves, by-pass, 7
  non-transfer, 6
WHEEL—
  alignment, 33
  bearings, 37
  removal,
    front, 35
    rear, 37
Wiring diagrams, 108–114

OTHER MOTORCYCLE MANUALS AVAILABLE IN THIS SERIES

ARIEL WORKSHOP MANUAL 1933-1951:
All single, twin & 4 cylinder models

ARIEL (BOOK OF) MAINTENANCE & REPAIR MANUAL 1932-1939:
LF3, LF4, LG, NF3, NF4, NG, OG, VA, VA3, VA4, VB, VF3, VF4, VG, Red Hunter LH, NH, OH, VH & Square Four 4F, 4G, 4H

BMW FACTORY WORKSHOP MANUAL R27, R28:
English, German, French and Spanish text

BMW FACTORY WORKSHOP MANUAL R50, R50S, R60, R69S:
Also includes a supplement for the USA models: R50US, R60US, R69US.
English, German, French and Spanish text

BSA PRE-WAR SINGLES & TWINS (BOOK OF) 1936-1939:
All Pre-War single & twin cylinder SV & OHV models through 1939
150cc, 250cc, 350cc, 500cc, 600cc, 750cc & 1,000cc

BSA SINGLES (BOOK OF) 1945-1954:
OHV & SV 250cc, 350cc, 500cc & 600cc, Groups B, C & M

BSA SINGLES (BOOK OF) 1955-1967:
B31, B32, B33, B34 and "Star" B40 & SS90

BSA 250cc SINGLES (BOOK OF) 1954-1970:
B31, B32, B33, B34 and "Star" B40 & SS90

BSA TWINS (BOOK OF) 1948-1962:
All 650cc & 500cc twins

DUCATI OHC FACTORY WORKSHOP MANUAL:
160 Junior Monza, 250 Monza, 250 GT, 250 Mark 3, 250 Mach 1, 250 SCR & 350 Sebring

HONDA 250 & 305cc FACTORY WORKSHOP MANUAL:
C.72 C.77 CS.72, CS.77, CB.72, CB.77 [HAWK]

HONDA 125 & 150cc FACTORY WORKSHOP MANUAL:
C.92, CS.92, CB.92, C.95 & CA.95

HONDA 50cc FACTORY WORKSHOP MANUAL: C.100

HONDA 50cc FACTORY WORKSHOP MANUAL: C.110

HONDA (BOOK OF) MAINTENANCE & REPAIR 1960-1966:
50cc C.100, C.102, C.110 & C.114 ~ 125cc C.92 & CB.92
250cc C.72 & CB.72 ~ 305cc CB.77

LAMBRETTA (BOOK OF) MAINTENANCE & REPAIR:
125 & 150cc, all models up to 1958, except model "48".

NORTON FACTORY TWIN CYLINDER WORKSHOP MANUAL 1957-1970: *Lightweight Twins:* 250cc Jubilee, 350cc Navigator and 400cc Electra and the *Heavyweight Twins:* Model 77, 88, 88SS, 99, 99SS, Sports Special, Manxman, Mercury, Atlas, G15, P11, N15, Ranger (P11A).

NORTON (BOOK OF) MAINTENANCE & REPAIR 1932-1939:
All Pre-War SV, OHV and OHC models: 16H, 16I, 18, 19, 20, 50, 55, ES2, CJ, CSI, International 30 & 40

SUZUKI 200 & 250cc FACTORY WORKSHOP MANUAL:
250cc T20 [X-6 Hustler] ~ 200cc T200 [X-5 Invader & Sting Ray Scrambler]

SUZUKI 250cc FACTORY WORKSHOP MANUAL: 250cc ~ T10

TRIUMPH (BOOK OF) MAINTENANCE & REPAIR 1935-1939:
All Pre-War single & twin cylinder models: L2/1, 2/1, 2/5, 3/1, 3/2, 3/5, 5/1, 5/2, 5/3, 5/4, 5/5, 5/10, 6/1, Tiger 70, 80, 90 & 2H. Tiger 70C, 3S & 3H, Tiger 80C & 5H, Tiger 90C, 6S, 2HC & 3SC, 5T & 5S and T100

TRIUMPH 1937-1951 WORKSHOP MANUAL (A. St. J. Masters):
Covers rigid frame and sprung hub single cylinder SV & OHV and twin cylinder OHV pre-war, military, and post-war models

TRIUMPH 1945-1955 FACTORY WORKSHOP MANUAL NO.11:
Covers pre-unit, twin-cylinder rigid frame, sprung hub, swing-arm and 350cc, 500cc & 650cc.

VESPA (BOOK OF) MAINTENANCE & REPAIR 1946-1959:
All 125cc & 150cc models including 42/L2 & Gran Sport

VINCENT WORKSHOP MANUAL 1935-1955:
All Series A, B & C Models

COMING SOON IN THIS SAME SERIES:

BRIDGESTONE FACTORY WORKSHOP MANUAL: 50 Sport, 60 Sport, 90 De Luxe, 90 Trail, 90 Mountain, 90 Sport, 175 Dual Twin & Hurricane

BRITISH MILITARY MAINTENANCE & REPAIR MANUAL:
Service & Repair data for all British WD motorcycles

BRITISH MOTORCYCLE ENGINES: By the staff of "The Motor Cycle"

CEZETTA 175cc MODEL 501 SCOOTER MANUAL & PARTS BOOK

VILLIERS ENGINE WORKSHOP MANUAL: All Villiers engines through 1947

www.ingramcontent.com/pod-product-compliance
Lightning Source LLC
Chambersburg PA
CBHW070555170426
43201CB00012B/1848